Hitchy Feet

To all the long-suffering fools who prop me up with kindnesses. You know who you are, and there are many of you.

Hitchy Feet

A grown-up's guide to running away from home
and accidentally getting a life

John Card

FINCH PUBLISHING

SYDNEY

Hitchy Feet: A grown-up's guide to running away from home and accidentally getting a life

First published in 2014 in Australia and New Zealand by Finch Publishing Pty Limited,
ABN 49 057 285 248, Suite 2207, 4 Daydream Street, Warriewood, NSW, 2102, Australia.

15 14   8 7 6 5 4 3 2 1

National Library of Australia Cataloguing-in-Publication entry:

Card, John, 1975- author.
Hitchy feet : a grown-up's guide to running away from home
and accidentally getting a life / JohnCard.

9781925048179 (paperback)

Card, John, 1975-
Men--Australia--Biography. Life change events--Australia.
Hitchhiking--Australia. Australia--Description and travel.

920.710994

Edited by Karen Gee
Editorial assistance by Megan English
Text typeset by Pier Vido
Cover design by Jo Hunt
Printed by Griffin Press

Contents

kick off

I taught a kid who went to jail for setting a human on fire. I remember a boy crying in front of the whole class because his dad was an arsehole; another kid delivering the eulogy at his mother's funeral. A boy who went from robbing houses to becoming a chef and a father; a girl who moved into pornography.

I used to work hard and enjoy the job. I remember a student called Sarah saying that it wouldn't matter what I taught, all the kids loved my class. It rolled off her tongue without hesitation. It was a teaching gold medal, unrecognised by others but glorious in my heart. I recall a mother saying that her son hated science last year and she didn't know what I'd done, but he loved it now. I recall a boy staying behind to tell me he had voices in his head, another telling me that his dad bashed him, a girl telling me she couldn't stop scratching her arms.

'Are they itchy?' I inquired.

She looked at me. 'No.'

But teaching kids was killing my enthusiasm for life, draining my energy. It was an occupation I had started to describe as boring. I had told the same stories and taught the same lessons. I'd seen five million drawn dicks and heard every semitone on the fart scale. My nose for a smelly classroom was numb, much like a sewerage worker who can no longer smell poo.

In my early years of teaching, I consistently declared that I had 'fallen' into the occupation, as if it was a hole. Perhaps I was pretending it was an accident on my way to becoming the Dalai Lama. In the last few months I'd thought about my existence as a science teacher. I'd even begun tuning into the staffroom noise in an attempt to discover what my life would become in the future. Like the background radiation of the universe, it resonated at a low whine.

It was time to do something else. I'd always been a bit of a talker, so I applied for two post-graduate broadcasting courses. I had little to no chance of getting accepted, but what the heck, there was no harm in getting rejected. This being a high possibility, I started to contemplate other occupations. With my minimal skills base, it would have to be a variation on teaching, like surf instructing or tour guiding. Neither of these excited me, so I pondered a recent idea: hitchhiking around Australia. I understood that hitching wasn't a new job, but that's what made it so appealing. Hitchhiking, however, was a lie. I wouldn't have the usual excuses: lack of money, suspended licence or mental disorder. I was middle class, polite, semi-organised and owned a car. It would be embarrassing and deceitful.

If I committed to the idea of hitchhiking around Australia, I'd need to sell it to my parents for two reasons. Even though I was thirty-three years old, I still wanted their approval and when I ran out of money, as I surely would, I would need theirs.

My mother was the key parent to convince – I would need to exploit her weaknesses. She'd written a book, was a member of a book club and read like her life depended on it. The strategy would be to inform her that I would write a book about the experience. When my money ran out, she'd have enough faith in my motives to provide fiscal assistance. Then I'd drink it all and ask for more. Perfect, except for the fact that the hitchhiking idea *was* ridiculous.

I was watching TV one night musing over it all when it occurred to me that the embarrassment of being a hitchhiker was a minor issue in comparison to my ever-shortening fuse, bleak outlook and general disenchantment. I cast my mind back to previous hitchhiking trips: singing *My Girl* next to a country road in Western Australia; sleeping under the stars on the Great

Australian Bight; smoking pot in the mountains and laughing hysterically about nothing. Simple and wonderful. Hitching could be a lifeline, but it wouldn't be easy. There always lurked the shadowy possibility of being pack-raped by truck drivers or eaten by Ivan Milat's cousins.

Still, I didn't scrap the idea. I'd hitched as a young man; I could do it again.

My dad walked into the lounge room and kicked me out of his chair. I was living with my parents again, near Ballarat in Central Victoria, which served as a reminder that I wasn't a real person. My mum was in the kitchen, making me a Milo as if to prove it. I've often wondered what it would be like to be my parents, dealing with my constant need for attention and ridiculous ideas. I hoped they would support my hitchhiking.

I told Dad. He enthused about it because he had hitchhiked when he was young. Mum laughed at my idea, thinking I was joking. It was time to enact the strategy. I suggested that I would write the story down, maybe develop it into a book. My tactic worked and she jumped behind the idea. I told her that I might be pack-raped. She just smiled and said, 'Character building.' Now I laughed. It occurred to me that a book on hitchhiking would struggle to capture today's readers, unless I included sex-starved prostitute vampires and shape-shifting biker penguins. I didn't dismiss the writing idea, though. Still looking for parental praise, I reminded my parents of the applications for broadcasting courses and that it would be easier to get community radio experience while I was hitching through Queensland. Mum smiled, handed me the Milo and said that they would support whatever I choose to do. I sipped it, thinking *I will hitchhike a lap of Australia and fuck the consequences.*

A week later I brought it up with my girlfriend, Laura, who was also a teacher. When the initial bluster abated, she voiced concerns about my trip turning into a six-month bender. I thanked her for the suggestion and said I hoped so. In the end she was supportive, which must have been difficult for her as she'd already been tolerating my hobo inclinations for some time. Further to this, I suspected she had doubts about the attainability of my goals and the suddenness at which they had come about. To write a book and become a radio announcer was a long shot. I approximated it would be three months before I saw her in September, then another three months before I saw her at the end of the trip. When informed of this, she didn't give me the high five I was hoping for.

1
Death roll

Two months later ...

Before I could even open the door and stand by roadsides for weeks on end, I needed to pack a bag. I flung everything into a pile: beanies, sleeping bags, shorts, scarves, boots, sneakers, thongs, thermals, board shorts ... What I chose to place in my backpack would be wrong and regrets were certain.

'Mum,' I yelled, 'will you pack my bag?' No response.

When I finished, I shrugged my shoulders. This would have to do.

On the day I was due to leave, memories of past hitchhiking incidents came back to me. I started getting nervous about the trip while Mum searched high and low for her car keys. I thought about the times I had stood for six hours without a lift; nearly been killed by drunk drivers; stood in hail and slept by the road.

All of a sudden I felt too old for such hardships. My mum, my gorgeous mum, found her keys and gave me a lift to the local train station and I caught public transport to my kick-off point on Melbourne's outskirts.

When I reached my first hitchhiking spot I turned, faced the traffic and waited. Standing there, I quickly became bored. Bugger.

Ten minutes elapsed before a ramshackle, late 1990s Hyundai pulled over. Walking up to the side of the car, I could see it was inhabited by a very large Indian man with enormous goal keeper hands.

'How ya going, mate? I'm John.'

'Rakesh.'

He shook my hand and it disappeared.

Rakesh was headed to work and I hopped in. As we drove along I detected that he was the type of gentleman who answered questions with questions. It was the sort of humility I'd craved in students for the last ten years. He was a divinely lovely human. We soon pulled up at his workplace, a Subway restaurant just off the highway.

I ran to the Subway door and opened it for him, adding a thankful bow, which immediately made me feel stupid. I took the opportunity to nip into the toilet for a quick whiz. When I emerged, Rakesh was already changed and behind the Subway counter. He must have been wearing his uniform underneath his clothes, like children do with pyjamas. He certainly hadn't had enough time to properly wash his hands. I stood gawking until he lifted his hand and waved. A bacterial wave. *Filthy*, I thought. Then, feeling guilty, I questioned my middle-class sensibilities. How could I judge him like that? I wasn't even sure his hands were dirty in the first place. I waved back, while watching him scoop up a 6-inch sub. It looked like a dinner roll in his big hands: a dinner roll of death.

As I walked back down to the road, I contemplated my attitude to Rakesh. In my young life I loved to think I was open-minded. In Year 8 I'd made friends with Slava Ha, just to prove it. I watched documentaries about Aboriginals on the ABC and was friends with girls and black people. But there was a strangeness to it, as if I was only meant to be friends with white Australian males who liked football and made jokes about wombat sex. In the end I became a teacher to demonstrate how much I cared. But what was I trying to prove? I didn't have a clue. And now here I was, bucking the trends and trying to be 'worldly' by standing next to a highway in Wallan, Victoria. I began to worry that I might be achieving 'wankerly' instead.

A Bible basher, a builder, an antiques restorer, the Hume, a pub. Ten hours. I was in Sydney.

2
Backpacker

Having arrived in Sydney after only one day's hitching, I settled into a bunk at a backpackers hostel and googled 'hitchhiker murders' on my laptop. My search found plenty of evidence that indicated I was at risk, but also a study that showed people feared hitchhikers. I imagined the same people were scared of biscuits and curtains. My googling was disturbed by a ranting Italian called Jeremy. As the backpacker tradition dictated, we became instant friends, wandered out to a bar and got drunk.

The next morning I struggled to deal with my hangover. Although I hadn't been insanely drunk, I'm old and was suffering so the prospect of making polite chatter in people's vehicles was horrid. Instead, on only my second day of a full 15,000-kilometre hitchhike around Australia, I decided to cheat by catching a train. It's not unusual for me to cheat; it brings contentment. My love affair with this dark art has gifted me a lack of any genuine skill in life. I can't do maths, interpret dance, play cards, use computers, make solutions, cut cloth, sew or operate instruments. I had always cheated my way to passing anything and collected no personal growth along the way. There is, however, the obvious ironic exception to my skill shortage: I'm a brilliant cheat.

At the cheaty train station I wasn't exactly sure where I was going, but I took a seat in front of a ticket seller and asked questions. The train to Brisbane cost $90 and the wait was six hours, which seemed alright. 'Brisbane, thanks mate,' I said.

Stepping out of the ticket office into Sydney Central Station, I looked around. The high wrought iron ceiling and never-ending floor tiles combined with business shoes to produce a clip-clopping echo. It made the space feel far busier than it really was. I scanned from face to face, as I had been doing since I was a boy, assessing emotional states for no other reason than habit. Backpackers sat in groups waiting to be transported north. They weren't playing hacky sack, swallowing fire or anything amazing, they simply looked content (and a bit dirty).

3
Fraser

After a train ride, two lifts and 48 hours I was on the pavement in Hervey Bay, Queensland. I raised my arm to wave goodbye to my latest chauffeur, Tony. He began to say something out of the car window, so I aborted my wave and listened.

'When you hitchhike on Fraser Island, avoid lifts from four-wheel drives rented by backpackers,' he said.

He was telling me to avoid them due to a high risk of accident. It was a charming sentiment – a keenness to protect a stranger from unknown dangers. Regardless of the warning, I would take lifts from backpackers. I would take lifts from anybody.

I was in Hervey Bay because I was planning to complete the 90-kilometre Great Walk on the neighbouring Fraser Island.

I had been doing arduous bushwalks for years because I believed they 'purified' me. In reality, all they have ever done is put distance between me and a beer fridge.

At six the next morning I boarded a ferry to Fraser Island and wondered upon matters of life and death. I began to question whether a solo walk was an intelligent choice. What if I broke my leg, was bitten by a snake or attacked by dingoes? Nobody could save me.

Once off the ferry I dropped in to the tourist office and asked the lady behind the counter some questions to allay my fears.

'How big are the dingoes?'

'About the size of a small border collie,' she replied.

That assuaged some fear, but when I enquired if dingoes hunted in packs, she said, 'I don't know.' I took that to mean 'yes' and started shitting myself.

To leave the Fraser Island town of Kingfisher Bay, I opened a 'dingo fence' (Fraser Island towns have fences to keep out the dingoes) and stepped into danger. During the first hour of walking, any noise from the bush sent me scampering forward, fearing for my life. No purification yet. During the afternoon I came across a hiker who told me to relax because dingoes only attacked little kids. 'Good,' I replied. I arrived at my campsite that night in a decent mood, having dropped any thoughts of dingoes.

The next morning I was out on the track early, smashing out kilometres. By 11 am I was nearly at my lunch destination when

I looked up from the track to see a tall, nude, redheaded male hiker yelling at me. He was conveying that he needed a moment to put on clothes. I faced away until he was decent.

'Havin' a nude stroll, mate?' I asked.

'Yes, it feels so free to walk without clothing. You should try it.'

I told him that it wasn't for me, but I thought that people should do what they want without being judged. That seemed to please him. 'Ja, ja, for sure,' he replied. He was Dutch. I had always imagined Europeans were nude in stylish ways: on yachts, drinking tea or playing boules. Not hiking. Still, I found hiking nude classier than Australia's version of nudity – running blind drunk across sporting ovals then crashing into goal posts. I paced away wondering why I was unable to abandon myself and strut around the bush stark naked. *Maybe I should be less of a prude. Maybe I could do it ...*

Three hours later, fully clothed and with no chance of disrobing, I noticed a scaly creature lying across the track. My initial alarm caused me to career backwards into a fern, snapping off a couple of fronds. After some deep breaths I took a closer look. It was an attractive diamond-headed snake with a short body. Despite my noise the snake remained glued to the path, so I threw a stick at it. It wasn't bothered. I threw another one. Nothing. Thinking it might be dead, I grabbed a stick and poked it. The snake wriggled, sending me hurtling skyward, screaming. I must have woken it from torpor. The deceitful bastard made me jittery enough to give it a wide berth through the bush.

I arrived at Dilli Village, my night's camping spot, and described the snake to the campground supervisor.

'Geez, that might've been a death adder.'

'Sorry?'

'Yeah, a death adder.'

I didn't feel clever. I'd poked a death adder with a stick. I was the Dilli Village idiot.

I lay on the grass in the campground enjoying my life, happy that I wasn't in an emergency ward skolling shots of antivenin. Or worse, slumped on the side of the track, dead from being stupid. I took off my shoes and played with my blisters. I rang Laura and told her about the snake. She laughed, reminded me to be careful and told me a story about one of her miscreant Year 8 students. Normal stuff.

The next day saw me rise early and begin a hitchhike along a long beach. I had walked 5 kilometres before a tour group in a four-wheel drive pulled over. People were jammed in the back along with the bags and there wasn't an inch for another human. The driver was a smiling, wild-haired young man. He was probably ignoring insurance policies, company charters and safety regulations – instant endearment.

'Jump on the back, mate,' he said to me.

It was a flat-backed troop-carrier and it was moving. My target area was a two-inch bumper. With 17 kilograms on my back, it was difficult to accelerate but I caught up, managing to grip the door handle and drag my foot onto the tow ball. It was nearly impossible to hang on, but there wasn't a choice: we were already going 80 kilometres an hour. The sea was flying along on one side and the bush on the other. The driver was taking pleasure in hammering through creek crossings and drenching me in water. I loved it.

I was in a boy's dream and the world was perfect.

When the driver dropped me at his turnoff point, I gave him a mega-grip handshake and the hard eyes of serious appreciation. My destination was still 20 kilometres away but I didn't care.

An hour later I was picked up and dropped in Happy Valley, still feeling brilliant. Happy Valley is an incongruous town in an otherwise undisturbed wilderness. It was weird to see houses, shops and a petrol station.

I walked straight into a bar and ordered a celebratory beer and a steak sandwich. The young barman, who had a rakish mop of blond hair and the build of an up-and-coming rugby star, grunted rudely in reply. A little confused as to what the grunt indicated, I stood for a moment, wondering. In slow motion he turned towards the fridge and shuffled forward. Was his dawdling designed to annoy me? Did he have a physical disability I hadn't detected yet? Or was it the actual pace of his work? Baffled,

I took my beer and sat down at a table. Not long after this he asked me to move tables, on account of a tour group coming in. When they arrived and didn't sit at the table I'd been forced to leave, I became agitated. An inner voice was demanding answers: *Who raised this boy? Why is he so annoying?* I was fixating on this bloke and in all likeliness staring at him unnervingly. I picked up on him laughing sarcastically at a tour operator's joke. My mouth began teetering with smart arse remarks but I gained control and remained neutral. His sarcastic laugh caused a ripple of laughter amongst the people in the tour group, so not five minutes later he did it again. I was beginning to realise that he didn't suffer from a disorder or disability – he was *just a massive wanker.* He sprang a question on me.

'Are you on your seventh or eighth day?'

'I'm only walking for five.'

'Most people take seven or eight days.'

'I'm taking five.'

He looked at me as if I was lying. I took the map out and began to show him how I was undertaking the Great Walk by hitchhiking up the beach to make it a loop.

He said, 'You're not doing the proper walk then.'

'No, I am. It's just ...' and he walked off in the middle of my sentence.

I regretted that I didn't follow him and make him apologise for his rudeness. I'd let a moment slip past that I should have addressed. I was now thinking how awesome it would be to belt him over the head with a chair.

When he walked past again I demanded that he look at the map and see that I was in fact doing the whole walk. After my explanation he simply said, 'Right,' and walked off. I was seething with rage but bundled it into a dark ball and moved on.

I stepped back into the wilderness and trekked along, annoyed that I'd let a genuine idiot ruin my mojo. It was a repeating story: always happy until somebody got under my skin. Maybe it was why I liked my own company so much. I arrived at my lakeside campsite at dusk, raced through my tent set-up but was beaten by the dark. Cooking under the light of a head torch, I felt my face soften with the contentedness of a simple task. The exhaustion stilled my mind, blanking it and setting it free of worry. After an alfredo packet pasta, I grovelled into bed, happy to rest my worsening feet.

Lying there, I cleared my throat and started telling stories to the bush. It felt pretty weird at first, but then I got into it, editing and retelling until I thought they sounded alright. I wondered if they were good enough for the radio. Closing my eyes, I was sublimated into dreaming.

During the night I awoke to the sound of paws padding outside the tent. I settled my breath to a controlled quiet, listening to a dingo moving about. It walked up to the end where my head was and gave me a sniff through the tent nylon.

Its nose was a foot away from mine. I prayed it wouldn't understand the thinness of tent fabric. After snuffling about for five minutes it walked unhurriedly back into the bush. I strained my ears to hear it, but it travelled a near-silent path through the stillness.

The next day was to be a big one: 30 kilometres to Lake Wabby. I rose early and hit the track at 7.20 am. Mornings in the bush can be unsettlingly beautiful. Sixty-metre tall trees were interlaced with thick vines. Giant palms shaded the forest floor, keeping it cool and pleasant to walk through, up to a point. After 20 kilometres my ambulation was carried out with the stoop of a 90-year-old. My feet were looking like minced pork, my socks soaked in blood. After 28 kilometres, with only 2 kilometres left, my groin started to object to my unnatural gait and cause the sort of discomfort that makes you laugh. When I finally reached my destination and took a seat on a wooden platform, my sigh of relief was spectacular.

That night I slept like I was sinking into the soil, enveloped in earth. When morning came I drew in a motivational coffee and attempted to raise enough energy to finish the walk. I covered the remaining 23 kilometres without wilting from the pain of my scabby feet.

When I came across the dingo fence at Kingfisher Bay, the finishing point, I was so elated you'd have thought I'd been emancipated. I ate a triumphant hamburger then caught the ferry back to the mainland. Standing on the deck, I stared down into the clear water and felt fantastic. A voice interrupted.

'Hello there. Are you going back to Hervey Bay?'

'G'day, sorry mate. Didn't recognise you with your clothes on.'

The Dutch fellow and I chatted like two blokes might after long, solo walks.

Once off the ferry our conversation continued in a pub. We sat sipping beers and staring across the water at Fraser Island's forest. The nudie Dutchman's name was Tom and he came from a country so flat, cold and boring this must have felt like heaven to him. I imagined him settling down, later in life, with his nudist family near a windmill. Perhaps he'd be a professor. Fraser Island would never be far away from me, but it would be a world away from him. The drunker we got the more we rationalised life. I told him that we are genetically programed to root, make babies and die. He was more circumspect, suggesting humanity had the ability to change and dictate the terms of its own future. 'Bullshit, mate,' was my reply.

We got drunk enough to head to a nightclub. I normally loathe them on account of the noise, but mega-drunkenness dulls both hearing and logic. With my blisters I danced like Peter Garret walking across hot coals, a style that motivated a Hervey Bay local to offer me a chair.

Tom knew it was time to leave after seeing me take microsleeps in my hands. Staggering out the doors we walked towards McDonald's. In the line I decided to chat to a bloke – 'Hello, how's your father?', that sort of stuff. He took umbrage and nailed me with a headbutt that put me on my arse. I looked up at the McDonald's queue in shock and confusion. My palms faced upwards in the manner of 'please explain', while my nose acted as a blood geyser, showering my pants and shirt. The offender was jogging off into the night, elated with his violence. I stood up like a bouncy monkey, all arms, legs and anger, ready for pursuit, knowing the whole time that I wouldn't follow through. In fact, if Tom had not chosen to stop me, I think I may have just nipped around the corner and hid behind a bin in case he came back.

Why didn't I chase him down and kick him half to death? After all, all he had was surprise. I'm fairly sure that I was stronger, harder and more motivated, but I couldn't do it. My past too often catches up with me; my inability to turn the corner and trounce the deserving is inexcusable. That bloke should have been put in hospital and while I knew I could do it, I didn't. Was I a better man or a pussy? I was that scared young kid in high school, rolling over again. I hated myself for it.

I felt as if I had a natural aversion to violence, but it didn't matter what I thought, somehow, violence would find me.

4
Fourteen

Daniel stood over me, holding my neck. Malice flashed across his face. My back was arched over a rail and my spine shrieked. The drop below me was 20 metres and I was at his whim and mercy. Then he let go and went to class. Just like that. I slunk off towards Latin but took a moment to turn, and watched him walk away. I'd have loved to bludgeon him with an axe handle.

Daniel was at the bottom of the pile academically. I understood his anger and used to feel sorry for him, but his chokey coping mechanisms killed any sympathy I had. His actions were part of my rejection by the Year 9 'in' crowd during 1989. I was confused as to why unpopularity had found me and analysed the past to work it out. I pinpointed an incident when I was playing football with about thirty kids.

We split into two teams. A bully organised to have all the good players on one side and the rest on the other. My sense of social justice found this an issue, but I didn't say anything. The game unfolded and my reject side remained goalless.

When play stopped I confronted the 'winners' about the injustice. People stopped and watched me lose my shit at a popular kid called Peter. He was one of those kids whose status stemmed from good looks – lucky for him, as he was a bore. I hated him. He jumper-punched me so I crashed my fist into his jaw. He counter-punched to my mouth, making my lips stick to my braces.

'You're a pharking karcok scucker,' I told him.

The 'cool' gang roared with laughter. I walked off towards the school gates, thinking about a permanent exit.

Arriving at the toilets instead, I looked in the mirror and pulled my lips away from my braces, causing both tears and blood to flow. I hated those dickheads and wished death upon them. At the first-aid office, I wouldn't tell the nurse what happened. I couldn't dob. That night, Mum and Dad asked me why my lips were swollen.

'Footy accident.'

In maths I sat next to a guy called Tank. His head was square, as were all his features, and he had deep-set eyes. Tank was the sort of human you could smash in the face with a shovel and he'd say, 'Is that all you got?' One recess, Tank and I were 'play fighting' because I had no choice in the matter. He kneed me hard in the nose. I staggered out the door, dripping blood all over the carpet in the stairwell. Stars blinked through my vision and my head thumped. Again, I lied to the nurse, then later to my mother and father. This was a shame I had to bear alone.

My breaking point was pressing in, but I was averse to falling to pieces in front of Mum and Dad. I needed to beat this. The answer came to me when self-sorrow turned to anger. I vowed to become stronger and flog Tank.

My dad had a set of Weider weights, which were made of a blue plastic filled with concrete. I might have asked Dad why he hadn't bought iron weights like everybody else, but I knew the answer. He was a tight arse.

Every night after dinner I'd start pumping concrete. Lying down on my milk-crate bench press, I'd smash out repetitions. Eight to ten was the best number for muscle gain according to the weight set's booklet. I'd strain, grunt, fart and groan my way through half an hour, thinking it would turn me into Arnold Schwarzenegger. I didn't realise he did weights for eight hours every day. I hadn't read that part of the booklet.

After a few months I became fanatical enough to dream of becoming a professional bodybuilder. By the time Arnold was sixteen he was competing in contests, so why couldn't I? I asked my dad if I could go to a bodybuilding contest.

'You want to pay $20 to watch men with big muscles and small underpants dance around on stage?'

'Yeah.'

His laughter was my answer.

After four sets of weights my little body would be vibrating. I'd vibrate all the way down the hallway to where Mum, Dad and my five siblings were watching TV. I stood in front of the TV set and cracked poses, declaring I was *massive*.

'Get out of the way,' they'd say without laughing.

I'd crack more poses while grunting my way out the door.

But, no matter what I did, my body seemed to stay the same: shapeless and weak. My lack of muscular progress made me wonder if I had an allergy to getting big, or if I was a physical misfit destined to be bullied till the day I died. Tank would be safe for a while yet.

5
Animals

In Year 9, my bedroom floor was usually littered with debris. On any given day you could find Lego men, gum leaves, apple cores, banana peels and dead animals of all varieties. I once counted fifty dead blowflies, three dead spiders, two cockroaches and a ladybird. After a holiday, I even found a dead bat under my bed.

Outside my room a koala occasionally resided in a magnolia tree. *What's wrong with a fucking gum tree?* I'd think. My dad told me it was a female koala. I told him he was a sicko for looking that closely. In the dead of night she used to bellow mating calls that sounded like she wanted to whore herself out to every horny marsupial in the district. One night she woke me from my dreams with the stridency of a car alarm. The noise went on and on until I decided to do something about it.

Walking out the back door of the box room that adjoined my bedroom, I screamed into the darkness, 'Shut the fuck up you furry cunt!'

'Hoy, don't speak like that,' Dad yelled from his bedroom.

'Sorry Dad, it just won't shut up.'

He was already snoring again by the end of my reply. Back I went to bed, but as soon as I hopped in Blinky Bill's whorish sister started up her slut routine once again. I got out of bed and walked outside onto the gravel under the magnolia tree. I scavenged about for a rock. I launched one into the darkness from where the sound emanated. It missed, and landed on the roof of the house. Bang, clatter, clatter, clatter, and into the gutter it went.

My dad yelled out, 'What the fuck are you doing out there, John!'

'Not swearing,' I said.

The Animalia festival did not stop with the whorish koala. The adjoining box room had a door that allowed outside access. It meant that I didn't need to go to the toilet to take a piss because it was only eight steps from my bed to an open door. Every living thing within piss radius of the doorway got obliterated. It was like I was actually pissing herbicide. No plant survived my lazy man's weeding.

Under that box room lived a blue-tongue lizard. It was a cute little thing. Waddling in and out from under the step, it would look around for food, glancing up at me, unbothered. One afternoon I spied the creature sunning itself. I snuck out onto the step so it wouldn't notice my arrival. Pulling down my pants, I let go of a golden arch that landed square on the back of its lizard head. I cracked up laughing. Not only was I dominating the kingdom Plantae with my herbicidal hot piss, but also the kingdom Animalia with my pesticidal penile poison. I was a god. The lizard scurried back under the house.

I thought it was so funny I told some girls at school the next day.

'Last night, after school, I pissed on the head of a blue-tongue lizard.'

'Oh, that's weird. How did it get in your toilet?'

'It was outside.'

'That's disgusting! I hate it when boys pee outside.'

What I found most unusual was that the girls found peeing outside more disdainful than pissing on a reptile. Among the lot of us, it was difficult to work out who was more bizarre.

That Saturday my mum demanded that I clean my bedroom, among a list of other things she wanted me to do. It annoyed the shit out of me – being handed a little bit of paper with eight thousand jobs on it. Cleaning my own room was a challenge. That was unless I shoved everything in the cupboard, which I did, every time. The next item on Mum's list was usually to vacuum my bedroom. I hated this task.

In order not to incur the wrath of my mother I began vacuuming my room. I'm not sure if it was the whirring sounds or the vibrations of the Volta, but I became very aroused. Aware of the fact that nobody was home, I released Percy the Penis for a view of the outside world. Percy's head was so swollen it looked as if it had gigantism (or at least the miniature version of it). I happened to be getting the dust out of the bedroom corners at that moment. This meant the head of the vacuum was not attached. Instead, just a round hole remained. Just for the craic, I let it have a short suck on my knob.

Vrrrmmmhhhppphhh it went on my doodle.

The feeling that whizzed through my body brought me to my knees. I was unsure if I'd just had some sort of lovely hernia or bizarre, momentary but pleasant liver failure. Whatever the fuck it was, it felt awesome. So I did it again and the same incredible feeling materialised. So I just left it there, whirring and sucking away. My whole body was shaking, as if I'd just suffered an electric shock. I felt like the filthiest, dirtiest boy on the face of the planet – but it didn't stop me.

My worries were but a minor distraction. My mind had transferred its powers to my two hairy brains. They were thinking about Carmel, a girl from school. She had delightful tits and a wonderful snatch … or so I imagined. The chances of me looking at her naked were a million to one. In my fantasy, she was the vacuum, and I was rogering her with the zest of a wild dog.

I lay on the ground in the throes of ecstasy. Then stuff came out the end. To be honest, it was completely unexpected. I really didn't even know what that gooey stuff was. I was in a state of shock. My jizz had zipped up the vacuum cleaner. The rest sprayed itself liberally over the carpet. Later on, when I realised the white goo was sperm, I momentarily pondered the possibility of a little baby vacuum cleaner. What went on in my mind was beginning to frighten me. I sat on the carpet with my wang all gooey and looked up at the window. I imagined the whore koala and the golden-shower-loving lizard cracking up laughing. I drew the blinds.

It would have been only about twenty minutes later when the shame had finally left me that I flicked on the switch for round two. I must be up to round 400,000 by now, but most have been unassisted by carpet-cleaning aids.

The following Monday I saw Carmel at school.

'Hello John,' she said.

'Hricmpakh yerp ah,' I returned.

She giggled at my mortification. If only she knew she'd been a vacuum cleaner on the weekend. No doubt she would have reported me to the police.

When Mum bought a new vacuum cleaner the next year I took careful note of its curves and attachments. Maybe it could be the love of my life?

6
Surfing

Sunshine was skidding off the surface of the water. It was 3 foot and glassy at Lorne. My dad was flashing the car headlights. That was the predetermined sign: we're leaving, so come in. It was amazing how long I could ignore those lights. This was my space. I loved it.

A wave bobbed up on the horizon. I paddled to the peak of it, swung around and jumped to my feet. I shot down along the wave, managed a shallow bottom turn and guided the board up and down the face. The water was rushing up it, chhh-chhhering behind me. The wave was closing down so I positioned my board, climbed up onto the lip and floated down as it broke. Amazingly still on my feet, I raised my arms in the air like I was Mark Occhilupo. Then lying on my belly, I cruised all the way to the beach. Smiling and feeling wonderful, I asked Dad, 'Did you see that last one?'

'Yeah, you're getting good,' he told me.

'One day I'll surf Pipeline.'

'That's great, John,' he responded.

That was enough to make me feel magical.

Sitting in the car with my head rattling against the window, I retraced each wave. The positioning of my feet during take-offs was too far forward so I visualised leaping to the correct position over and over and over and over. *Throw your weight back*, I'd tell myself. I rolled my back into the seat, arcing a cutback. I needed to twist harder to throw a bigger spray, drive a higher line to generate greater speed and use a rhythm by swivelling my shoulders in four-four time.

Outside of school, sitting in swells, I was my own man. It gave me confidence and a dream to hang on to. At school I was learning to lose myself in my imagination. I was barrelled in hallways, floated down steps, ripped snaps around corners and stalled in alcoves.

Dreaming was a gift. Dad used to say, 'Don't set paradigms for yourself,' by which he meant break the pattern you're in. If he'd crawled inside my head, he would have known that my imagination allowed for limitless potential. I knew it was only fantasy, but sometimes I'd let myself go for five minutes before crashing back to reality … *maybe I could be a good surfer*. This was my sport, it represented me. I was somehow over the idea of being a bodybuilder anyway. My love for a revenge sport had morphed into an obsession for a therapy sport. No bullies in my ocean, just waves and skills.

In the car on the way home I'd drift off to sleep. The waves would break in my dreams. I'd be the champion.

My parents, who'd been running a country pub, decided to move into a home-building franchise in 1989. The recession then hit and destroyed their company. Fortunately for me, it necessitated my leaving the private school I'd been at and attending another institution. Although at the time I thought it would be fantastic to leave Tank and Daniel, I worried that my life at a public school would be worse.

Mum, Dad and I discussed the different options. The worst case scenario was East High and it frightened me senseless. In order to survive there, I would need to wear ball-hugging short-shorts; lose three teeth; get inked and grow a long mullet. (Mullets were the barometer of disadvantage – the longer, the tougher.) I worried a lot.

During my summer holiday I began to investigate the possibility of a transformation. Tattooing was the first port of call. I found an engraver in the shed, dipped it in ink and pressed it against my skin. When I turned it on, it felt as if I was stabbing myself. Ink sprayed all over my new Quicksilver T-shirt and I kicked the bench in frustration, nearly breaking my toe. Tattoos were out. Going inside, I found a pair of my younger brother's school shorts and squeezed them on. I stood in front of the mirror and looked at myself. I could see the faint outline of my balls. The shorts accentuated my fleshy white legs which, in combination with my curly long hair, made me look like Nicole Kidman. I'd be sodomised during my first class. I gave up and played with the dog.

The summer wore on and my parents were hoping to get me into the best public school in the region, Ballarat High. I was taken for an interview with the principal, Gonzo. I knew being accepted into the school was important to my parents because Dad wore his shiny brown shoes and Mum dressed in her flowing skirt like she was Scarlett O' Hara. On arrival, Dad exuded confidence and joviality while Mum was quick-witted and to the point. They never failed to impress strangers.

Their polite conversation with Gonzo annoyed me because two evenings before, Mum had been screaming at Dad for his his miserly appreciation of her ironing. Now they were projecting that everything was smelling of roses. *Phoney hypocrites*, I thought.

In my interview, Gonzo looked through my school report. I was worried because I'd only achieved twenty-eight per cent on my Latin exam. My parents had encouraged me to do Latin, which right at that moment must have felt silly to them. Gonzo didn't comment. Maybe he accidently missed it. It occurred to me to stand up and draw attention to that fact. I'd tell him that it was healthy to be aware of one's own faults – but I was shitting myself and didn't say anything.

My head was running all over the place and maniacal thoughts wove through my cerebrum. *Fuck, I'm being too quiet. I'm no different to a student who has had a tractor run over his head. Maybe I should dribble on myself.*

Then a question was fired at me.

'What would you like to do when you get older?'

I couldn't say watch television, surf and go on the dole, so I said to Gonzo, 'I'd like to go to university and study geography.'

Now who was the phoney?

In the end, with my parents' charm and my false tertiary intentions, they let me in to that school. I had no idea what to expect, but I was relieved it wasn't East High.

When the first day of school came I put on my green uniform instead of the brown one and I went to the coordinator's office. There I met Mr Quick, a tall, friendly man with comfortable brown eyes. He gave me a timetable and a diary and told me all sorts of stuff that I didn't absorb, mainly because there was a nervous poo in my pants. He walked me to biology and presented me to the class. My new peers stared while I wriggled on the spot, hoping for spontaneous combustion.

'This is Mr Nickaluc.'

'Hello, Mr Nickleck.'

Laughter rippled across the class. I went the colour of a stop light and sat down. Mr Nick started talking and I started listening. He showed the division of two growing placental cells. I found it amazing that meiosis and mitosis had made me. I liked it.

During my first-ever recess at Ballarat High I stood at the bottom of the locker steps. What was I to do, walk in circles? There was no pre-determined pattern to follow like there had been at my previous school. I didn't know where to hide. A boy called Joe Righetti came over and saved me, taking me over to meet the sporto-heads. They were jibing each other about their results in the local cricket competition. They paused and asked me questions and I answered them carefully. I'd been a bullied flop at Ballarat Grammar. Now was the time to consider how to integrate myself into this school.

My answers must have seemed like a weakness, as a boy called me 'octopussy head'. My fringe was longer than the rest of my hair.

'Watch what you say … dickhead,' was my reply.

He looked taken aback and didn't say it again. In the same group there was another new boy who was telling stories and being outrageous. I could see trouble unfolding, so I surreptitiously suggested that he understand the terrain before choosing the vehicle. He dismissed my advice. He should have taken it – it was only a matter of weeks before he'd found his niche as a punching bag. Not me, I was making friends.

Finding a social slot was delightful and a little too enticing. Getting laughs and having fun seemed acceptable in this school. It was my forte at home, so I ramped it up. I developed routines of bullshit and by the latter half of the year I was kicking back, working my way towards being the number one class clown.

One day during English I'd been sat at the front of the classroom – it was my enforced location and beyond boring. Ms Bolterod laughed at my jokes but didn't appreciate the interruptions. The phone started ringing in the coordinators' office nearby and the class stopped chatting and listened.

'Do you want me to get that, Miss B?'

'Oh yes,' she said sarcastically.

Before she had time to stop me I was off and out of the class. I picked up the phone.

'Hello?' I said.

'Who's this! You're a student, aren't you?'

'The coordinators are not in right now, can I take a message?'

'Who's this? What are you doing in there?'

I hung up. *Oh fuck*, I thought, *maybe that was bad*.

I walked back to the classroom. The class was silent and focused on me.

'Well, who was it?' someone asked.

'Mum,' I said.

The class roared with laughter and I sat back down in my seat, stoked at having caused a giggle.

I was beginning to love school. The difference between schools was amazing. The absence of wholesale snobbery at Ballarat High was a reason for joy. No longer would I have to deal with insults about the yellow Mazda van my parents drove, nor did I have to tolerate stories of skiing in Europe for family holidays. People in this school drove ten-year-old Toyotas and camped at the beach for their holidays. Most of all, I was free from bullies. It's hard to describe how fucking beautiful that was.

7
Taxing

I was leaving the backpackers in Hervey Bay to start hitchhiking again when four injured Poms walked through the door. They looked pretty bad, certainly worse than me, with my blackened eye and sore nose from the headbutt at McDonald's. One of them told me that their four-wheel drive had tipped over on Fraser Island and one girl was still in hospital in critical condition. Tony had been right. It was dangerous.

After a long day of hitching I was left in the dark at a roadside camp just outside of Gladstone on the Queensland coast. I settled down for a good night's sleep. When I awoke at dawn, I lit a small fire to cook breakfast. Heating up my pita bread to the point of frailty felt like art. I snapped it in two and placed two Kraft cheese sticks in the middle to melt. I surveyed my surroundings for the first time. A wide river flowed 200 metres west of me at the bottom of a steep slope and was bordered by mud banks. I looked for crocodiles but couldn't see any. At the roadside stop there were ten or so four-wheel drives with attached caravans that had camped overnight. Grey nomads were pottering about like birds looking for seed. I greeted them with perfunctory nods, bitter because they never gave me lifts.

I could see that the highway was roaring with half-empty cars and I yearned to get on it. I began packing but was interrupted by a tall wiry man wearing a loose-fitting singlet. He had sinewy muscles and a big, thick head. He told me his name was Phil and he was from the Cook Islands. I looked into his dancing brown eyes and the pupils indicated that he'd been on the borderline of psychosis many times.

'The Goods and Services Tax disables Australians of their sovereignty,' Phil said out of the blue.

'Why's that?' I enquired.

'It's like the VAS in England.'

This was not the answer to my question and, in any case, he was wrong.

'VAS … Do you mean the VAT?' I asked.

'Yeah, the VAT. Yep, it's exactly the fucking same, hey!'

It wasn't. I like acronyms to be right and Phil had chosen the abbreviation for Vaseline, which evoked masturbation, not taxation. I was grinning about it until I realised Phil wasn't.

I stopped smiling and enlisted an anti-violence tactic … I agreed
with him.

'Yeah, bloody government can't leave us alone, can they?'
I answered. 'I don't feel sovereignty with that tax. Not at all!'

He had such a mad look in his eye that I would have agreed
if he'd said Benjamin Netanyahu was Palestinian. I manoeuvred
the conversation elsewhere. 'So, are you here with your family
Phil?'

Phil pointed out a twelve-year-old boy 50 metres away.
The boy was bashing vegetation with a stick and I figured he'd
inherited a similar mindset to his father. He was absolutely
bashing out his sovereign future.

Phil started telling me about bringing up his boy. According
to him, he was a firm and fair sort of father but allowed
his young fella a little bit of room here 'n' there. When Phil
wanted to get pissed at the pub, he made his twelve-year-old son
drive.

'Oh, right. Good driver then is he, Phil?' I asked.

'Yeah, he's okay. But he let me down once, the little bastard.'

'How's that then?'

'Ah, instead of picking me up from the pub first, he took the
piss by joy-riding 80 kilometres out to Launceston, collected his
mates, then came to get me, the little shit.'

Phil looked genuinely annoyed by this recollection. I thought
he was worried for the safety of his son.

'Yeah, used a fucking tonne of petrol,' he said.

Phil blithered on and on before I found the courage to say I had to go, and off I went to hitchhike in waning traffic.

Next to the road I noticed a line of ants crawling along the gutter. Just ants, I thought vaguely to myself. I looked up and noticed Phil's twelve-year-old son meandering over, swishing his sovereignty stick.

'Did you take your old man's car to Launceston, tiger?' I asked. He didn't seem in the least surprised that I'd started our conversation with an invasive question.

'No, I drove around the bush but never to Launceston.'

Oh, I thought to myself. *Somebody's lying … but who?*

The boy pointed to the ants at my feet. 'Check out the fire ants.'

'Fire ants?'

'Yeah.'

'Like the ones that bury and eat you?'

'Yeah.' He put his hand in front of the line of marching ants.

'Are you sure you want to do that?'

'They only attack if they think their nest is threatened.'

Considering I taught science, I felt I should've known that. I didn't. In an attempt to regain a little pride after seeming so ignorant, I asked, 'How do you know one of them doesn't have bipolar and will misjudge your intention?'

'What?'

It appeared he didn't know everything. It felt so good re-establishing my intellectual superiority over a twelve-year-old. No wonder I'd given teaching the arse.

When I'd finished chatting to Phil's kid, a Commodore pulled over and I left my little campsite next to Gladstone. Inside the car was a man named Dean. He was driving all the way to Townsville, 1000 kilometres away.

'Fucking awesome,' I told him.

8
Bar

'Good luck getting a gig on the radio,' Dean yelled as he drove off.

'Cheers mate.'

My 1000-kilometre lift to Townsville was made in record time and I found some accommodation at a backpackers, which was to become my home for eight weeks.

I spent the next day walking around, checking out the streets. Each street seemed to have a palm tree, a bloke with a neck the same width as a palm tree and a shiny car that said, 'I like motorsport above all things, including my wife.' The vegetation generated its own tropical hum. I was worried that if I poked at it, a bug would shit chlorophyll in my face.

In the same road as my accommodation I noticed a sign that read 'Triple T', which I assumed to be a community radio station. In order to be accepted into the broadcasting courses I'd informed my mother about, I needed some practical experience. I promised myself that I'd walk in there the very next day, introduce myself and beg for some opportunities. I had to, otherwise it was teaching till death.

That night, I made friends with a German man who cajoled me into skolling goon juice like I was fifteen, not thirty-three. The German pointed to the ingredients of the goon, which showed that it was made with fish and eggs. This should have put me off but it only livened my spirits because I was now eating dinner at the same time. After an hour or so we headed to a bar in the centre of Townsville. Seeing a disco ball, I ran directly to the dance floor, cleared some space and performed a slow forward roll to amuse my new friend. The bouncers witnessed it and turfed me out onto the street, where my drunk-compass helped me stagger in the direction of my backpackers.

Not many steps into my walk, the police asked me to get in the car with them. At that stage, I just thought they were friendly police who would run me back to my accommodation.

Incorrect.

They were arresting me. When I was informed of this I said, 'Really?' as if they were a comical police service.

The arresting officers were polite, as if they were dealing with an intellectually disabled child in the presence of its parents.

At the police station I was asked to stand at a line and take off my belt.

'Really?'

'Yes, mate. Really.'

Then my shoes, hat and the contents of my wallet were laid out before me and my money counted out. It suddenly occurred to me that prison is where bum-rape occurs.

'Can you put me in a cell by myself?' I requested. 'I'm middle class, a school teacher, not some ruffian.'

The woman police officer assured me that I would not be thrown in a cell with a real prisoner. I was going solo.

'Oh, thank god,' I told her camply.

I was asked to hold up a board and pose for a photo. I tried my best hard-man face but was finding all this so much fun that I was struggling not to smile. Next I was taken to the cell area.

The bed, which was essentially a bench, was made with a plastic material that I'd be unable to rip to pieces and fashion into a noose. There was a metal toilet bowl positioned behind a low concrete wall. Above the loo was a security camera, so the police could watch me wee. It felt pretty perverty, but I guess I was in a prison cell, where actual perverts sometimes resided.

I sat down on my plastic mattress and contemplated how many people might have shat on the bed as a protest to their incarceration. I stood up and looked through my perspex window down the hallway. A heavy-set man with tattoos on his neck was being escorted to a cell. Two officers had his arms pinned tightly behind his back. When he caught me staring, he pulled one hand free and gave a friendly wave and smile. I stupidly turned around to check if there was a prisoner behind me. No. I was the prisoner the hooligan was attempting to befriend. To him, we were like two kids in after-school detention. In complete fear, I gave him a wave back. Christ!

I lay down on my plasticky poo bed and attempted to sleep so as to awaken to release. I was too cold to nod off so I yelled out to the police. 'Hello, excuse me, can I have a blanket please?' I had used my manners, just as my parents had taught me. A blanket was promptly delivered. My dad often said that good manners will open doors. I would be sure to tell him that it wasn't always the case. After passing it through the gap to me, the officer spotted a 'this is not as funny as I thought it was' look on my face.

'You'll be out in the morning. Everything will be fine.'

'Cheers for the blanket, you're a lovely police officer.'

'No worries.'

I wrapped it around me and went to sleep on the plastic bench.

What seemed like shortly after, I was startled awake by a banging at the door. 'Oi, hey. Wake up.'

'Errrr, yerr, yes, er.'

'What's your address?'

'Um, it's one of two.'

'So, what is it? Out with it.'

'328 Musterngaurd Road, Musterngaurd, Victoria 3441. Or alternatively, RMBM 328 Musterngaurd, Victoria 3441.'

'So, which one is it?'

'Oh, the post will go to either one. It works either way. The postie knows us.'

This officer didn't seem in the least interested in my friendly relationship with the local postie.

It was about 8.30 in the morning and I was delighted to be freed from my cell. The morning police were far more gruff and more 'policey' than the night crew that had arrested me. They counted out my money and asked me to stand on the line. I was accustomed to it after having had a 'don't go over the line' moment during the previous evening. In fact, I clearly remember trying to pre-empt their instructions as a sort of need to please, student-to-teacher scenario, sad bastard that I am.

As I walked towards the door, I noticed the height scale for the line-up photo. I leapt in front of it and gained the attention of the two officers behind the desk.

'Do you think I've grown from the experience?' I asked.

They didn't raise a smirk but I laughed at two things: my own joke and the fact they didn't laugh. They may have been repeating an internal mantra: 'I officer, me good. Him prisoner, him no good.'

Walking out into Townsville's morning sunshine, I glanced down at my release form and noticed the space for my address had 'unknown address' written in it. I laughed like any other loon leaving a police station. I learnt one major thing from the experience: being in a prison is like being in any other room in the world, except for the empty space where the door handle should be.

When I rang my mother and told her about it, I was still drunk. She enjoyed my ranting about the waving psycho with the neck tattoo, the lack of door handles and the forward roll that got me incarcerated. In fact, she laughed quite a bit, meaning she wasn't particularly ashamed of me, which disturbed me. I rang my girlfriend Laura and she was shocked and angry.

'Why are you angry?' I asked.

'You were locked up!'

'It was only for a bit.'

I didn't care because I'd been expecting to go to prison since I was fifteen. I figured that I was a credit to myself having lasted twenty years outside. My real question was, 'Will I ever go again?'

Two days after serving time I walked into Triple T, the Townsville community radio station. I met Leonie, the receptionist, and asked how I might get on the radio. I was very nervous.

Leonie told me that I needed to speak to Norma, because she was the manager. When Norma appeared, I ranted at her about what an amazing person I was.

'I've hosted trivia for corporate events and I've been the longest-running trivia show host for Quizmeisters Trivia.' Blah, blah, blah.

After my burbling she responded with, 'You've got a nice voice.'

That calmed my nerves. Norma explained that there would soon be a Monday night training session and I was welcome to attend. I thanked her for her time and bobbed out into the street singing, 'I've got a start. I'm a man with a start. I'm the dude with a big massive start swinging between my legs, like a giant start of startyness.' Then into: 'I'm a firestarter, a lipstick firestarter.'

A couple of days later I went in again and asked which Monday Norma was talking about.

'Not this one coming, but the next,' I believe she said.

'Oh.' My lipstick firestarter had been doused a little. I began to explain the urgency of my situation. 'Actually, Norma, I'm attempting to get into a radio course either in Western Australia or Melbourne. I've got a bit of a timeline that I need to work to. Is it possible to get involved a little earlier?'

I was smiling in a pleading way. She told me that she might be able to help me and invited me to sit in on her show starting in half an hour. Within fifteen minutes of the show starting, she asked me to read the weather and community notices live on air. My heart thumped so hard in my chest I worried I might crack a rib. It was great to be nervous about something again, I could hardly remember the last time.

Over the next couple of weeks I became adequate enough to go to air with my own show, *Daybreak with John Card*. I enjoyed playing the tunes but the show lacked a lot. Talking to carpeted walls is not the easiest way to create entertainment. I decided I needed to do some prank calls. I called Channel Seven News in character as a bogan.

'Hello, Seven News, Dan speaking.'

'Yeah, g'day mate. How ya goin'?'

'Good, how are you?'

'Good mate, I'd like to read the news, mate, if possible. I'm getting bothered by Work for the Dole. Is there a chance I could read the news?'

'Ah, I don't think so, mate.'

'What about the weather or somin' like that?'

'Ah, why don't you come in and try to sort something out?'

'So, just come to the front desk and say that I'm here to read the news?'

'Yeah.'

'I've got a criminal record n' that. Will it bugger things up?'

'No, no.'

'I've got every opportunity n' that?'

'Yes, absolutely.'

'What do you do down there, mate?'

'Okay.'

'What do you do down there mate?'

Beep beep beep.

I didn't play it on air, instead I rang back and apologised to the guy. I didn't want the sack at Triple T just yet.

I then decided to do some co-hosting, so I asked Andy and Dave, some newly made Irish mates, if they'd like to join me in the radio station one morning for a recording. They both agreed, and on a Saturday morning after a beer or two we trundled down to make some radio.

The first pre-recorded show went like this.

'The Irish are well known for being alcoholics,' I began. 'Are you guys alcoholics?'

'Yes,' said Dave.

'Have you ever thought about dealing with your problem?'

'No.'

'So that's it then.'

'That's it. I'm quite happy with it. It's part of our culture and people expect it of us and we have to deliver that.'

Andy piped in. 'It would be a shame to let them down, really.'

'Now, Andy, do you ever drunk-sleep on the street?' I asked.

'I have been known to sleep on the street from time to time. It's not very cushy but it's sometimes … where I tend to fall.'

We went on like this for quite some time. On review of our chat, I'd have to say it was awful, but it was awful in the right direction. The main thing I worked out from getting Dave and Andy on my show was that I laughed. That proved to be important.

Each night I'd work hard sourcing material for the following morning. I'd find the typical stories about one-armed boxers and alcoholic elephants and rant like a complete dickhead. I didn't feel super-confident and I didn't really enjoy it that much. I hoped it would be fun when I got to work with somebody else, a co-host. A mate would be the greatest solution. Laura listened to my show on the internet. She said I was good. She had to, she's my girlfriend.

Was I mad to be pursuing this? I couldn't see anything else playing out so I continued on. I hoped to be one step closer to living the life I wanted.

9
Chooks

I'd been in Townsville for five weeks and I was on radio, but I was still unemployed. Martin, a big Swede I met at the backpackers, had been going off to do all sorts of crappy jobs while I was pursuing my radio stardom. The one that amazed me most was his job as a chicken farmer. When he first told me about it, I looked at him as if he was the solitary cataclysmic carrier of anti-RSPCA sentiment.

'So, what do you do again, Martin?' I asked him.

'Vwee get za chickens out of one cage and put them in another cage.'

'All day?'

'Yez, all day.'

A week later, I checked my bank account, cried, then took off to an agency to sign on for chicken farming. It stunned me just how many forms you need to fill out to be a mover of chickens. They wanted to know previous addresses, my level of education and hat size. The ideal form for such employment would have asked two questions: 'Are you hopelessly broke?' and 'Are you a human?'

When I finished I was told to watch a safety video and do a test. I passed and they asked me to begin work on the following day.

There were five of us: Martin, Alex, Dave, Andy and me. After driving for 30 minutes we saw massive corrugated iron chook sheds rising out of the trees. We arrived at a spot where there were around thirty to forty people standing about. My mates and I joined the throng and I tuned into a variety of accents, nationalities and personality types: Filipino refugees, Italian studs, Manchester rabble, Australian Jim Beam drinkers, Aboriginal fluorescent-jacket wearers, French beauties and Irish lackeys. The strangest thing was the number of really good-looking girls. One was about nineteen and from somewhere in the north of England. She spoke like a tramp on tramp steroids, but she had an arse like an arse on arse vitamins. I could hardly wait to see how she responded to a shed full of chickens.

We were given a short lecture on handling chickens.

'Listen up,' said a little Filipino fella. 'You are to work 'ard all day. You need to treat chickens right. Anybody who bashes the chickens will be arksed to leave.'

I recognised an easy way out if I couldn't handle the job.

The Filipino went on: 'First we will be movin' all chickens out of one shed, then into another. Some people will be putting the chickens in the cages and some people will be taking them out.'

This was difficult to conceptualise. Chickens in and out of cages. I was waiting to hear the correct way of handling them as if I was in an ornithological lecture. No such information was given.

'Okay, everybody on truck, let's go.'

We all got on the back of an open-tray truck and searched for something to hang on to. When the dust settled we found ourselves looking at a gargantuan squawking shed. The smiles of the girls in the group faded slightly before those of the boys. We were marched down rows of cages to take our positions. This alone was harrowing. On each side, not 30 centimetres from each ear, were chickens bawk-bawking madly. They leered at us and any sudden movement caused an enormous cavalcade of sound. With the smell, noise, claws, beaks and beady eyes, I'm amazed I didn't just leg it.

In front of me was a trolley into which I was to stuff chickens. On my left were 30,000 chickens to choose from. All I had to do was stuff them into a cage on my trolley. I opened a tiny gate and the chickens retreated. Martin had told me that the best way to move them was to grab them by the legs, but the chook I had chosen leapt over my hand and stood with its arse pointing at me. I made another lunge at its legs and tried to drag the chicken slowly out of its prison. I looked up to see Martin watching me, smiling. He had four chickens in one hand and two in another. My bird, in the meantime, had taken to using its wings like arms, grabbing at the steel frame. I folded its little arms back and inserted it in the back corner of the trolley cage.

Number of chickens in carrier trolley: Martin – eighteen; John – one. I hated being beaten.

I loaded up the top of the trolley first. This meant that the chickens were eye to eye with me. Most of them were cowering in the back of the cage as I searched to jam more in. However, as I spun around to deliver the eighth chicken into the trolley cage, I saw that another chicken had ventured to the edge of its new home and was bending its legs. It leapt straight at my face. I twisted sideways to avoid it but it clawed me down the side of my cheek and climbed onto my head. I slapped it off and stood back, slightly stunned, a trail of blood running down my neck. It had taken off for the freedom usually only ascribed to a free-range chook. My brain is 400 times larger than a chicken's brain, yet this particular one was strutting away victorious. I found pleasure in knowing that my species would eventually triumph over that smart-arse chook by hacking her into bite-size pieces and feeding her to a fat kid.

The first hour actually took at least four. Time warped backwards and sideways as I tried to get used to grabbing birds in that noisy, stinky environment. When the first smoko arrived there was a general sense of relief all around. Standing in the shade of an old tree, I told a couple of Irish blokes about my mission to hitchhike, write and get on radio. They stared vacuously into the distance and drew long and hard on their cigarettes. It appeared they didn't give a shit. Their demeanour was so intense I wondered if they were contemplating how many kilograms of Semtex they needed to do a proper job on the House of Commons. The hot Mancunian girl was still pumping about in her black leggings. If these chickens weren't careful, one of them would receive a rogering due to all the sperm this woman was creating in the flaccid, sweaty nut sacks of thirty-five backpackers.

It was in the third hour that we felt comfortable enough with the chickens to start pretending to deflower them. At any given moment you could look around to see a chicken giving a fake head job, another copping a shag doggy-stype – or should it be chicken-style – and occasionally an attempt at the ever-so-dangerous chicken cunnilingus. Strangely enough I bonded with the other backpackers on the 'sex with chickens' front. It broke down language and cultural barriers like no other form of communication. I wondered if Ban Ki-moon of the UN knew this. If not, maybe I would call.

The rest of the day plodded on. When it eventually finished we toddled off to the backpackers in the car. When we got back to the Civic Guest House, Irish Dave, who I had been working alongside, pulled four eggs out of his pocket.

If working with chickens was the sacrifice I needed to make to catch a break in a new industry, I could just about manage it.

10
How heavy are weights?

One morning my Irish friend, Dave, and I went shopping. Dave required new shoes and I had nothing to do. He searched Shoo Biz and I walked around the store, watching people. I saw a father wearing a designer T-shirt, thin-soled black canvas shoes and beige shorts covered in Pocahontas tassels. Out-dressing an Indian squaw seemed a tad excessive. His hair was glued into spikey curls and he was desperately attempting not to interfere with his son's choice of shoe. The son would pick up a shoe, roll it around in his hand then look up to see his dad subtly shaking his head. The boy was working his way towards a pair of black canvas loafers, identical to his dad's. When he picked them up, the father raised one eyebrow, tilted his head, wriggled his lip and nodded. It's the sort of quiet endorsement that looks mildly more interested than indifferent. The son was culturally clued in and knew the winning shoe had been chosen. He rolled it about in his hand to establish an element of independent decision-making, then nodded at his dad.

The bonding was nothing short of delicious and it forced me to consider if many blokes had been through the same shoe selection process with their dads. I couldn't recall one with mine. It was always Mum, a pram, a crying toddler and an unshakeable maximum price that wasn't enough to buy a shoe box, let alone a shoe.

The passing down of the vanity values by the Shoo Biz father was vexing. I'd always hated excessive vanity in youth. Plus I wasn't a fan of black canvas loafers on a thirteen-year-old boy. It made him look like he was heading to an over-35's nightclub to pick up ice-dabbling single mums. Maybe he was.

I'd taught thousands of boys and the ones without a dad (shoe savvy or not) were often unrealistic and difficult. Life would later teach them what their absent father hadn't. Seeing this situation was a gentle reminder that there were caring fathers everywhere. I could thrust the vanity issue aside because this boy had a father he loved. And that was enough to break my heart. The boy strolled off to the counter with his father, but not before shooting me a look that asked the question, 'Why is a paedophile staring at me?' I looked away, embarrassed by my stalking enjoyment.

I popped my head around the corner to check what Dave was up to. He was mincing about in a pair of average-looking Allsport shoes.

'What 'bout dese?' Dave asked me.

'Ah, I dunno, Dave. They'd look alright on a homeless man.'

'Tanks, John.'

He picked up another pair from the shelf. 'What ya tink of dese?'

I stared blankly back.

'I loik dem. I'm buying 'em.'

Dave was medium height, bald, fit, strong, hairy, with blue eyes, a round face and a love of confusion. He approached the lady at the counter and handed over the shoes he'd chosen. I moved into an expectant proximity.

'How yer doin? Are dese dem shoes for the ice skatin'?'

'Ah, I'm not sure that you can go ice skating in these shoes. I don't think so anyway.'

'Can ye put attachments on dem, you know … wid de blades n' dat?' Dave asked.

She turned them over to check. At that point I knew we were dealing with a girl who'd had her brain partly crushed during birth. 'No, it doesn't look like it,' she told Dave. But then she decided to get curious. 'Where are you going to do that? You can't go ice skating around here.'

'Toowoomba, in the equestrian centre,' Dave replied as quick as a flash.

'Oh, right,' she said.

I was contorting in violent mirth in the background. At what point would a normal person challenge an Irishman when he tells you he's going ice skating in a centre for horse riding in Queensland?

After the $19 shopping spree we returned to the backpackers and psyched ourselves up for our favourite excursion … a trip to First Choice Liquor. Dave, Andy and I had a profound enthusiasm for the establishment. When a new First Choice specials pamphlet arrived in the mail it was announced down the backpacker hallways like a call to face Mecca and pray to Allah. We'd pore over it, considering all the different ways we could get drunk on a budget.

On this occasion, Dave was very excited. 'Look at that, Wild Turkey only $34.99, or look – Carlton Dry slabs, two for $70.'

'Yeah, Dave, that's about turdy-tree euros each.'

'Turdy-tree and a turd,' Dave quipped.

When we arrived at the bottle shop Dave said to a sales assistant, 'I've never been in one of these alcohol shops before. Can ye help me choose?'

The woman, not sensing the sarcasm, told us, 'You've landed in the right place.'

We settled on a bottle of whisky then headed home and drank it within an hour. We decided to head to the pub.

'I'll go and get changed,' I informed Dave.

I reappeared in jeans, a beanie, a Norwegian jumper and swimming goggles. It was 28 degrees Celcius. The best I got from anyone was a wry smile, but for Dave it was an inspirational moment. He ran up to his room and returned in a suit and swimming goggles. We rolled our way down to Flynn's Irish bar in the centre of Townsville where inquiries flowed in.

'Why are you wearing goggles?'

'Protection from bats,' Dave said.

On leaving the pub, we slurred our way through a discussion of theft.

'What do ya wanna thieve then, Dave?'

'Weights, from da pool, ye know 'em, John. We've talked about this. Come on now.'

'Yer, righto,' I slurred.

We'd previously identified the location of some rusty weights that we saw as a trouble-free theft. Dave and I had talked about doing weights before, although I don't think either of us was serious.

'John, do ye lift weightsz?'

'No, Dave. I've thought about it, but they're too heavy.'

'Ah, dat id be a good point now.'

We moved off towards the pool, staggering about suspiciously, whispering and laughing. When we arrived on the perimeter of our target there was a thicket of dense foliage. We belted our way through, then Dave unexpectedly disappeared. The foliage had obscured a boulder-laden tidal channel. Dave was lying in the bottom making that sort of giggling that only funny bones can solicit.

'C'mon, Dave, this is serious!' I reprimanded him. 'We're proper criminals.'

Dave stood up, put on his stealth face and we laughed some more. At that moment we heard sounds coming from the footpath 50 metres away.

'John, get down. It's the Viet Cong.'

We tucked down low behind the bushes, only poking our heads out to see two other blokes staggering about the foreshore, probably looking for something to steal.

'Dave. Look … competitors.'

'John, have you still got your goggles? Put 'em on, then they won't be able to see us.'

'Right you are.'

We moved towards the pool fence. Dave led the way and I began to follow when a horrible pain hit me. It was a poo pain. Not an ordinary one: it was as if a small incendiary device had gone off in my colon. On my way down into the squatting position, I had to push Dave aside so I didn't poop on his shoe. It was a millisecond later that a Mr Whippy exited me.

'Well, you seem to feel pretty comfortable around me, John.'

'Yes I do,' I responded, laughing and pooing at the same time.

I didn't bother to explain to Dave that I'd been having this bizarre tropical problem where I sometimes needed to shit immediately. I looked around and saw a big monstera leaf that was serving as criminal cover and tore it into strips of leafy toilet paper. I was praying not to accidentally dip my bottom in my own poo as I rocked side to side with drunkenness. I looked up to see Dave busy at work, lifting weights straight over the top of the fence. I finished wiping my bum, then moved into position and picked one up.

'Fuck, they're heavy, Dave. Any lighter ones?'

'No, John, dis is all I can reach.'

'Fuck. Righto.'

We ended up staggering out of the garden bed with four dumbbells. We decided on the most inconspicuous route home, which would take us away from the main drag but unfortunately added about a kilometre to our trek. The toll of the weights on my arms was immediate.

'Dave, are we sure we need all of these weights? What about one each?'

'Keep going, ye'll be right.'

Up and over several small hills we pushed, through to our final street.

'Dave, I need a sleep,' I announced.

'Yer'll be right, John, not far now.'

The final street included the courthouse prison where I'd already been, the police station and a Centrelink office. This stretch of road was a highway to the danger zone of exposure. As we approached the courthouse, Dave started telling me stuff …

'Der's a car been circlin' twice 'bout us. I can 'ear it again, tis best we make for dem bushes.'

Our running style was severely hampered by the weights. We did a slow motion dive into the bushes. Dave lay flat on his belly and I crouched down in a higher, more dense section, peering out at the vehicle. It was a security guard. He pulled his car over opposite our garden bed and started to make his way in our direction.

'Shit Dave, he's coming right for us.'

Dave just looked at me drunkenly. 'Fuck, Dave, we've gotta run. We've got about twenty seconds. Dave, let's go now!'

Dave's face remained the same. He was doing this on purpose.

'Ten seconds Dave! I'm fucking going. Dave, you can come or not, but I'm going!'

I turned on my heel and leapt out of the bushes. Dave miraculously leapt from a lying position to running. We hit the afterburners. What the security guard would have seen was one tall man with goggles around the back of his head and one short man with goggles around the back of his head. We didn't turn around to show him our faces but we glanced at each other and roared belly laughter that could kill cancer. I giggled my way into the grounds of the local university with trillions of places to hide. Dave tore up a side street that led to Castle Hill, where he sat hiding in the bush. I carried on straight to the backpackers, hopped into bed and went to sleep.

In the morning when I awoke I moseyed over to Dave's room and slid open the door. On the floor were three of the four stolen weights.

'Dave, what did you do? Go back and grab 'em at five in the morning?'

'Yes.'

'Fucking legendary!'

And I lifted them up only to be reminded of exactly how cumbersome weights can be. 'Fuck. Why?'

11
Jam

At Ballarat High School teachers often said you are who your friends are, so I started to seek out the drug addicts and the criminals. My half-friends from Grammar (I don't think I had any genuine friends when I left) had been goody goodies. I loved the new types of people in the public system. Some of them were so wild. I was a kid in the candy store of marginalised humanity.

I became mates with a guy called Thommo. He had perfect blond ringlets hanging over his shaved undercut and big, blue eyes with a devious twinkle. He was so extraordinarily cool that I never witnessed him in an extreme state of any emotion, happy, sad or otherwise. He spoke as if he were commentating a surfing contest – one smooth word rolled melodically into another.

During one afternoon of schooling we were sitting together in human development class.

'Your uterus is located just about here,' Miss Best said as she indicated an area lower than her abdomen.

'Right, where I'm gonna stick my cock,' whispered Thommo.

'What are you laughing at, John?' Miss Best enquired.

'Nothing. Sorry, Miss Best.'

Her class was mind numbing and it prompted a suggestion from Thommo.

'Wanna wag tomorrow and do some robbin'?'

'Sure,' I said.

We started making arrangements. We needed a crow bar, a screwdriver, hats and transport. Hats were important. I'd seen Crime Stoppers. Thommo was delegated the task of obtaining bikes and I would grab Dad's tools. We decided to use our own hats.

The next day I caught the school bus but didn't go to school. I diverted to Thommo's. First up, we discussed lunch. Thommo thought I should make the sandwiches. I agreed, thinking that I'd be able to use my sandwich making to manipulate Thommo into doing the thieving graft later in the day: 'But I made the sandwiches! You should break the window.' He sat flipping pages in a catalogue and sipping a cup of tea. I buttered the bread then spread blackberry conserve thickly over the slices. It was just how I liked it. Thommo criticised the thickness of the jam. I told him that he could suck men's cocks for nutrition if he didn't like it. He chuckled then got focused on the order of the day. 'Where should we go to rob houses?' he asked me.

'Affluent areas.'

'Affa-fucken-what?'

I explained the word to Thommo and he responded with 'Let's go to Black Hill, there are loads of affluent rich fuckers up there.'

As we pedalled towards Black Hill I became wary of seeing police and kept looking around. We cycled until the houses got grander and backyards were filled with pools. I was carrying the criminal tools in my backpack, and with every scoping kilometre it got heavier. Cycling past a white house, I noticed an open window. I shouted at Thommo, 'There's a window open over there.' We skidded to a halt.

'Who's going through it?' he asked.

'It was your idea to be a criminal, Thommo. You do it.'

'Fuck off, Card, you spotted it, you do it.'

'But I made the sandwiches.'

We argued for another two minutes before I caved in and took off down the driveway. Thommo watched over my bike and when I turned around to get the all-clear to go through the window, I saw him eating a jam sandwich.

Climbing up through the window was easy enough, but clambering from a high bathroom window, head first, into a bath was not. I knocked over all sorts of body lotions, gels and soaps. When my feet hit the sink, leaving a perfect print of my shoe, I suddenly realised what I was doing. My eyes dilated, I became hyper-aware and felt a monster surge of adrenaline. I was up on my toes, cautious that a grown man might materialise and pound my face. Each new room caused more fear and more adrenaline. I felt amazing.

Standing in the lounge room, I looked around for something to steal. Family photos, trophies and a couple of kids drawings were all I could see. A moral reminder wasn't what I needed so I moved into the master bedroom. There was a TV, a lamp, two mirrors and a couple of paintings, nothing I could fit in my backpack.

Thommo and I had discussed this issue during class the previous day. 'Go for the VCR, cash box, camera or whatever the fuck looks expensive,' he'd suggested.

The VCR looked fancy so I unplugged it and took it out to the back verandah.

I tried to fit it in my bag but the top was protruding. I ran down to Thommo and asked if he could get the zip done up; he couldn't. The VCR was going to stick out like a sign reading 'Arrest us.'

Thommo insisted that I carry the backpack.

'I've just robbed the fucking house, Thommo, you carry it.'

'Na, man.'

I nearly hit him. So far he'd done nothing but eat jam sandwiches and stand near a bike. I felt sure he would have pinned it all on me if we were stopped by the police.

It was about four kilometres to his parents' house and we pedalled hard. We were making a right-hand turn on our bikes when Thommo made an error. He tried to turn across the street to go right but hadn't checked properly for cars and leaned into the door of a passing ute. He came flying off his bike and slid across the road, causing his hat to fall off.

'Faark!' I yelled, worried he had exposed his identity.

He lay there for a second, before limping to his feet with torn shorts and bloody knees. This was not the time to be having crashes, but after his lack of cooperation on all robbing fronts I wasn't that upset about it.

I rode up to him and asked if he was good.

'I'm alright,' he assured me.

It was hard not to be thinking about the VCR and the prison sentence while I inspected his wounds.

The ute had pulled up 50 metres down the road and a man hopped out to see if Thommo was okay. Thommo said he was going to scab money from him for a new pair of shorts. I could hardly believe my ears. We were mid-crime, standing in broad daylight with the loot and Thommo wanted immediate compensation for a crash that was his fault. This friend of mine was fucking unbelievable!

I urged him not to, but off he went. The meeting looked like it was going well as the man pulled out $30 and gave it to him. I'm sure Thommo would have haggled for more, but my urgent gesturing succeeded and we moved on.

Thommo and I cycled back to his parents' house and stashed the player under his bed. If we could get away with this, nearly anything was possible. The next day our crime was in the paper. I cut out the article and stashed it in my surfboard cover. Two days later we sat around talking about who we should sell the VCR to. We decided on a mate's rich older brother – surely he fancied some stolen goods? Fortunately he did and promised to buy it. He had only one question.

'Where's the remote control?'

12
Phil-istine

I stood tall in my school uniform and scanned the bus's carpeted luggage rack for my Toronto Blue Jays sports bag, but some bugger had moved it. I loved the bag because it was from my Canadian uncle and I thought carrying it around made me appear worldly. What's more likely is that it made me appear like an Australian who likes American stuff and there has always been a question mark over those individuals.

'Where's my bag?' I enquired generally to all the other kids on the bus.

Nobody said anything and I could feel all eyes on me as the bus remained motionless for forty slow seconds while I searched. Then a young fella whispered up to me, 'Phil hid your bag.'

Phil was the same age as me but he'd been kept down quite frequently. I used to joke to my bus mates that his school always tried to keep him in 'yesterday' but this sort of time-warping parallel-dimension quip never got a laugh.

I spotted the bag behind the air-conditioning unit, picked it up and walked up to Phil's seat. 'You're a fucking dickhead, Phil,' I said.

As I uttered 'dickhead' Phil was on his feet, reaching over his seat and trying to grab me. I leaned away and stepped off the bus. My brothers and sisters all looked at me.

'You're dead,' they heard Phil screeching as the bus doors closed.

'You're dead,' my brother Dave said to me.

'Thanks for the confidence vote, Dave.'

There would be a fight. My mental preparation started right then and there. If I was not to be bullied again I would have to stand up for myself, and in this case, I thought that meant teaching myself a boxing combination. How would I do this? I had no idea how to fight apart from the basic principle of swinging fists about. I needed to overcome a few hurdles – my lack of pugilistic experience, talent and equipment.

First there was the equipment. I needed to make boxing gear, so when I arrived home I searched for the materials to construct a punching bag. I found my grandma's toy stuffing, a spud sack, a shovel, garden gloves and soil. I shovelled loads of dirt into the bottom of the spud bag, jammed in the stuffing, found some rope and hooked it all up to the cypress tree in the backyard.

Standing back I felt focused. Looking towards the house, I saw my mum watching from the lounge room. Her facial expression implied I was beyond her now.

Most country boys' scraps begin with people grabbing hold of each other's collars and pushing and shoving. Mine was not going to start like that. I decided to follow a right hook with a left upper cut in a combination I practised until dark. Thump, thump in quick succession, over and over again. Lying in bed that night, the idea of a massive fight enclosed around me. Was Phil the sort of bloke who would kick me in the head when I was prostrate on the ground? Would he leave me a crippled, dribbling wreck until the end of my days? I didn't think so, but I didn't really know so I stayed paranoid and couldn't sleep. I hopped out of bed and gave my brother Tom a call to discuss my imminent punch-on.

'Tom, I'm going to have to fight Phil tomorrow. What do ya reckon I should do?'

'Punch the fucking life out of him and don't get into that pushy shovey stuff. Just hook the prick.'

Phil was on the bus in the morning. We exchanged menacing glances but no punches. Fights were for afternoons.

My school day was uneventful, but by period five I was nursing butterflies the size of magpies, and by the time I hopped on the first of my two buses I was distressed. As my destination approached I became unable to talk. Getting off the second bus was like stepping into the arena. It was going to be on.

My friend, Ian, walked next to me and my younger brother, Dave, was behind me. I could see Phil and his bogan mates 50 metres ahead. I handed my bag to my brother and marched along, ready for combat, repeating to myself *I'm going to fuck him up, I'm going to fuck him up*. When I stood in front of Phil he uttered some words but all I heard was, 'I'm a fairy princess from Narnia'. Words were converting to my violent overture. Adrenaline hit me in a huge wave. My eyes glazed over. This was another world.

In one step Phil was reaching for my collar. Dumb, predictable and idiotic. I grabbed his collar as a guide for a crashing punch to the jaw. Thwack. I cracked him a ripper. It caught him off guard. He covered his head with his hands and stooped forward. I was throwing upper cuts, trying to break through his arms to pound his head. One out of four was landing. My right hook/left upper cut combination had flown out the window and street fighter had stepped in. It was then that Phil made an unexpected move: by scrumming forward he was able to trip me up over a school bag.

Before I knew it, Phil was on top of me and I was in strife. But he had no time to throw a punch because I reached up, found his eye socket and rolled him off the top of me. Kneeling on his chest, I crashed a huge punch into his cheek. The spot turned red. Now I was the ringmaster. It was the first time I'd managed to have a good look into his eyes. They were wild, like a terrified animal. I leaned in and told Phil, 'I could fucking kill you.'

'Get off me,' he said.

I looked up from Phil and saw that I was in the middle of a stadium of adolescents. People were on top of the bus shelter trying to get a better look at the violence. It freaked me out. Standing up, I stepped back, keeping an eye on Phil in case he attacked. Phil stood up and made a tentative step forward.

'There's more if you want it,' I goaded, raising my fists.

Phil looked defeated and I walked away. Five hundred eyes watched me make my way to the next bus. I felt no pain from the fight.

Then *crack!* Phil had snuck up behind me and landed a punch right in the back of my head. It was as unimaginative as it was gutless. Swivelling low on one foot I swung around, grabbed his collar and started punching him in the head again.

I was mid-delivery when I was tackled by a bus driver and that was the end of that. He marched me off and I stepped up onto my bus. It was my first proper punch-on and the feeling was immense. I sat down next to a friend.

'Who won?' I asked.

'You did,' he said.

Phil hopped on the bus not long after. He probably wasn't going to hide my bag again. Not only had I succeeded in putting to bed a bully, but I had released a new confidence. I wished I'd taken to Tank and Daniel with the same vigor. If I had, I wouldn't have hidden in my own mind for the last couple of years.

13
Broken

My life has been littered with choices. After finishing Year 12 then working for a couple of years, I made the choice to start a Bachelor of Arts Social Science degree at Latrobe University. It was an incredible year for me. I was very concerned I'd be outwitted by geniuses and clever Larrys. Instead, I was clever Larry. I topped my geography class both semesters and did well in Politics and Sociology. It was mind-bending to find that I was capable of all this. But throughout the year my favourite moments were at parties or social evenings. I'd always find myself showing off — that was my true love.

After a year at Latrobe I had achieved quality results and was in a great position to make a smart choice. It was possible that I'd be able to transfer into all sorts of different courses. It felt as though the world, for the first time, had begun to open up a fraction. Careful consideration was required for my next move.

November of that year was the time to apply for a different university course and I needed to decide on the right one. To help me think it through, I took a trip up to my parents' block in the forest. Tree ferns, trickling water and the smell of sodden bush permeated my senses. I walked up a stream and past an old mine. I broke branches just for the fuck of it and found a high point in the forest at which to sit. I looked around me. The bush made me feel alive to possibilities. I stared at a wattle tree and noticed it had recently dropped its blossom while another tree, about five metres away, had not. I wondered why.

I asked myself *How does all this bush stuff interact?*

Later that week I decided to study Environmental Science, Natural Resource Management, at Deakin University. My dad was pleased with the decision because it was a Science degree. I wasn't to know the course content was drier than the Tanami wind, but it was my own horrible choice and the decision was made.

I started at Deakin, as I did everywhere else, getting in people's faces, looking for laughs and trying to find someone to hump. Although my daily actions suggested that I should take a course in dramatic arts or attempt stand-up comedy, I learnt about vascular bundles and phototropism.

On a Saturday night, with ten beers in my belly, I was at ease with the ridiculous, but I couldn't really believe that I could be a joker or a storyteller for a living. *I'm not smart enough* recycled in me like a little storm. You need to be clever to be an entertainer. I was just a boy from the country.

> He had the gun for no other reason than to hold it. He liked the feel of it in his hand. It was heavier in his palm and lighter at his fingers.
>
> 'It's the weight of lead power,' he thought, feeling slightly homicidal, but dismissing the thought as soon as it had come.
>
> He really liked the feel. The police were staring at him and yelling, '*Put the gun down!*'
>
> 'It's just really fucking heavy,' he said, smiling, nonplussed.

This is from a book called *The Outsider* by Albert Camus. This passage isn't a direct quote, but the sentiment of it stuck with me. The story is about a Frenchman who subscribes to an irregular morality. His style came to affect mine. His book was existential, a theory that essentially panders to desire or simply goes with the flow. It absolves the subscribing theorist of guilt and allows a morality of free will. It's an alluring concept to a 21-year-old university student; the doctrine that justified my hedonism.

Why the fuck not? became my line of logic. I often didn't consider other variables, just will and desire. I came to believe that, in the end, nothing really mattered. I believed that actions on this planet were largely irrelevant. This allowed me to insult strangers and surf more often than not. I was an existentialist, or just plain stupid … you choose.

The problem with my unofficial sign-up to this doctrine was my glaring hypocrisy about its vague ideals. I wouldn't and couldn't fundamentally commit to the theory. I wanted a university degree and I wanted to be somebody, but at the same time, I hated people blindly following rules both written and unwritten. It frustrated me into a personally damaging rebellion.

For a long time in my life I ebbed and flowed like plastic floating in a king tide. Taking control of my life and pursuing goals was a joke. If my clan tried to get through to me, I mocked them. I used a well-practised defensive voice so that nobody could guess my hopes and dreams. I was scared inside the veneer of my skin so I made myself emotionally impenetrable. The longer this went on, the more I despised not only myself but others. I grew cynical. I felt that people around me were obsessed with irrelevancies – garden chairs, seat covers, curtains, roof seals and hub caps. They seemed to ignore every opportunity for mind expansion. I concluded there were far too many cretinous buffoons on this planet.

The students at my university did not see knowledge as intrinsically valuable but as money. It grated on me. I could smell their greed; it seemed to be the fundamental philosophy of the masses. It popped up in conversations with new acquaintances.

'What are you doin' this weekend?'

'I'm working all weekend and looking around for a house to buy.'

'How old are ya?'

'Twenty.'

'What about sex on the beach, rock and roll, drugs and alcohol … you don't find any of that stuff tempting?'

'No.'

And so it seemed to roll.

People weren't searching for the truth; they were searching through Car City for a better Corolla. It appeared that no-one wanted to stand on a ridge and ponder the wealth of our natural history or political philosophy. They didn't want to sit in the middle of a rainforest and soak up the aroma of wet eucalypts. There wasn't a collective desire to feel Mother Nature's significance, only to exploit it. It made me wonder how we'd become so disconnected from what humans once were. I read about earlier civilisations, which helped me form a utopian picture of the past. I learnt about nomadic people, Aboriginal songlines and walkabout. It brewed ideas like tea in my synapses. I learnt that a naturally sustainable tribe was, for a long period, around one hundred and fifty people. This made sense to me because I could believe that in such a community belonging and caring would have thrived. Disenchantment and depression would have been circumvented before it occurred. Having children and the elderly around would create balance in life. I believed that society's sickness was spiralling out of control. It gave me reason to believe in nothing, but most of all, it led me to believe that *I* was nothing.

From what I'd seen of the projections and hopes of others, they made no recognition of the past. Great parts of me wanted to disconnect from what society was and from what I'd become: a senseless joker with nothing to add but silly remarks about how aliens would respond to a situation. I was a young man who craved inclusion and then rejected it, all in the one breath. I didn't know how to stay connected even if I wanted to.

Then I started to read Jack Kerouac novels and his life and travels quickly fascinated me. He'd shot a poison arrow of philosophy right through me. It twisted and turned and drove my madness. What was it about his writing that struck me? He moved, shook, lived, loved, hated, learnt, listened and kept his mind open. He got drunk and wrote about his life. Something was always happening in his books. He looked at others who lay in mental squalor and distrusted them, much as I did. He moved and learnt as I only dreamed of. His main character, Dean Moriarty, spoke realms of truth to my sponge head. He inspired me. I started hitchhiking a lot.

14
Whoops

I finished my three-year degree in natural resource management and didn't bother having my degree presented to me in an academic ceremony. I took a job as a water-meter reader immediately afterward and worked for as long as I could handle the boredom.

My girlfriend at the time suggested I become a teacher. 'A teacher!' I said. I weighed up my prospects – itinerant labourer or teacher? I wasn't able to see past a din of negative voices to find my path and teaching seemed to be my only option. I didn't have the talent to be a professional surfer and there was no such thing as a professional wanker – I would have been elite at this – so there was only teaching. As a student I'd been dreamy and never paid much attention to any teacher's postulations. The idea of standing in front of a group of children and telling them things was bizarre because I knew that if I was sitting there facing me, I'd not listen to a word I said.

It took some time for the idea to find footing, but when it did, it came in the form of a burgeoning messiah complex. So I moved towards teaching for want of a better option and in the vain hope that somebody might adore me. I didn't celebrate all that much when I was accepted at Monash University. My first thought was that at least I had something to do next year.

The course was useless, but at the very least my mother and father were pleased. Following my teaching diploma I got a job as a science teacher at a secondary college on the Mornington Penninsula in Victoria.

My first class caused an electrical storm to roll through my nervous system. The students stared at me with an air of expectation and I said words at them with absolutely no clue as to the ramifications of those words. Trial and error is the backbone of a good teacher – the more errors, the better the teacher. I tried to make all my errors during that first class so as to get them out the way. Unfortunately, the number of available errors was only comprehendible in Greek mathematical symbols. Trying to master the skills of teaching proved to be fun for a couple of months, but the job's challenges soon laid themselves down before me – more specifically, the behaviour of the students and my inability to love the work.

After six monthes I began to miss my ex/not-ex girlfriend, who was now in England. So I decided to fly to England, re-unite with her and teach in Manchester.

The second school I ever taught at was called Stanford High School. The name made it sound prim and proper. Lots of schools in Britain have lovely names and psychotic kids hiding behind them with knuckledusters and knives.

Stanford felt like one of the shittest schools on the face of the earth. The place was a floating mound of crap. The classroom allotted to me had featured on England's version of *A Current Affair*. During the week of filming, but not actually captured on tape, a kid shat in the teacher's desk drawer. In the same week an African refugee student named Josemar leapt from the classroom window two stories up to show how mad he was. The teacher present at the time hadn't managed to stop it. He broke his ankle. These were not prime conditions for learning. Needless to say, I wasn't going to make a difference. The only thing I could try to do was keep them in the classroom. I was a bouncer.

My classroom was a sewer and whenever the bell went, different shit flowed in and out. There were kids who were part of racist fronts, kids prone to random violence and an array of bullies. I hated many of them. They would posture and pose up to me as if they could batter me, and I had to crush thoughts of belting them.

Culture is a force and the culture in and around Ashton-under-Lyne, where Stanford was located, was pitiful. Alcohol ruled. Atrophied, angry single parents told their kids to 'Get the fuck out' as they got blotto every night on cans of lager. The kids were given freedom to roam, not because they wanted to but because home was horrible. This meant kids brought each other up. Often twelve-year-olds were getting drunk and having sex more often than me. Maybe I should have been jealous, but the reality was I felt a great sadness. My attitude to some of those kids was formed while I was clinging grimly to sanity. I was pushed and pushed every day in that system. It was difficult to take.

During one class a bully called Harrison sat in the back row smoking cigarettes under the table. I had been told that he was a member of the BNP, the British Nationalist Party, who are renowned for their racist policies and fascist ideals. I hated Harrison as much as I've ever hated anybody. During my class he set fire to a poster on the wall. As I stamped it out, I demanded that he leave the classroom. He didn't move. The class was cheering. I couldn't decide if he was taking pleasure in the notoriety or simply enjoying torturing me. One way or the other, if I'd left to get the principal I thought he would have set the whole place ablaze.

Harrison used to bully new students on their first day. Any Muslim kids would be called ragheads to their faces. My inclination was to hurl the little bastard out of my classroom, but I was getting £140 a day so I kept a lid on my anger. That day I was making my way back to the front of the classroom, edgy with rage, when Borhan Babic, a Serbian refugee, stopped me and said, 'Do you wanna know what I did last night?'

'What's that then?'

'Fucked your girlfriend.'

I didn't know what to say. I wanted to hit him.

'Borhan, get out,' I roared.

He strutted out of the classroom and I followed him, intending to bash the living fuck out of him. He leaned against the wall, smiling. I turned the corner and took rapid steps towards him. Raising my hand high in the air, I went to punch him but pulled up one inch from his face. He staggered backwards and his face changed. Fear flowed through his eyes. In this rage I felt masterful. As he continued backwards I took another step forward and grabbed him by the throat. He cowered into the wall.

'Look at me.' I said.

His eyes looked beaten.

'Listen to me, you little cunt. You ever fucking speak to me like that again, I will flog you to within an inch of your filthy miserable existence. I'll kick the living fuck out of you and love it. It will be the end of my teaching but I couldn't give a flying fuck. It will be worth it to see your ugly fucking head bleeding on the ground.'

His eyes grew bigger.

'When I come back to teach you tomorrow, you'll fucking do everything I tell you to without fucking thinking about it … you understand, Borhan?'

'Yes.'

'And?'

'I'm really sorry, Sir.'

Considering what I had done and the fact that I was the adult, asking him for an apology was ludicrous.

The bell went shortly afterwards. The day was over. Standing in the middle of the classroom, surrounded by paper spitballs and sound bites of profanity, I hated myself. It was as if I'd crossed a line too far to return from. In the heat of the moment I would have loved to kick a bit of respect into Borhan, but I knew in my heart that wasn't the way to make change. Admitting my violent longings caused deep conflict within me.

I felt teaching was not for me, that I had no self-control. What was next, punching a kid in the jaw? In no time I'd be in Strangeways prison getting my arse raped. That night I was lower than I'd ever been. Slumped at the table in my flat, I drank two bottles of red wine. Who the fuck was I? In Australia, teaching was easy, sometimes fun. Over here it was impossible. Hatred for English kids was slowly devouring me. I needed to stop, but the money was so good. This made it a little easier, but it had a shelf life. Maybe my time was up.

The next day 10B, Borhan's class, came into my classroom. They sat down noisily. It took five minutes to get them to listen. There is nothing more humiliating than having thirty teenagers ignore you. It taps at your self-worth like a jackhammer. Eventually I imparted the beginning of the lesson. The students needed rulers and without missing a beat, Borhan put up his hand. 'Sir, can I hand the rulers out for you?'

'You certainly can Borhan,' I said.

The expression on his face showed the effects of my anger. My soul was black. But he never did misbehave after that. He hung back to talk to me and chatted with eminent civility. It was bizarre. I hypothesised that his father must have beaten him. It was his language, what he understood. I'd shown him that I was a man, not afraid to lash out and demand respect. This made me feel like vomiting. Chances are, I'd frightened a kid who'd been hit for half his life. I was an empty vessel, a shattered glass. No better than a bully. The opposite of everything I wanted to be.

It never happened again – I had discovered restraint in a moment of madness. Maybe people need to walk the line to know where it is. That night I asked my girlfriend if she'd fucked Borhan, and she replied that she hadn't fucked a fifteen-year-old Serbian refugee.

'Oh, that's nice,' I said. 'Me either.'

We laughed but the pain remained in me. The situation seemed to me to be a reflection of the disrespect society has for adolescents. How on earth can jamming thirty kids in a small room with one adult truly mirror anything but disdain for our youth? How is society supporting its children? Where is it raising the bar? I didn't know. The loss of positive culture, the nuclear family and community means that teachers in rough schools are babysitters. They educate 9 per cent of the time and tread water the rest.

Who can live like this? Why is it so hard to get it right?

15
Sales

After nearly six weeks on air at Triple T, I wasn't too far off having enough recorded material to make a decent audition tape to get into a university course in radio. But I still needed more funds to stay in Townsville and continue my announcing on community radio. The chicken farming was intermittent and I really needed something permanent. The time had come to either work properly or perish. Approximately one month before this fiscal crisis I'd fired off my resume to a company called Dunk Sports, answering an advert for sports marketers. It was a little vague in its description of the work but it said sport, so I applied. I got the call for an interview.

Two days later I was sat on a chair only 2 metres away from the reception desk of Dunk Sports, where I waited, listened and watched the sort of idiots that might be my work mates. One dude was dressed in an Austar shirt, yelling 'Close … rehash … sell … sell' at his employees. I had to stop myself laughing.

Before my interview I was asked to fill in a form that required me to rate myself on leadership, punctuality, problem solving and motivation. The scale went as follows: poor, okay, good, very good and excellent. Grinning with conceit, I circled excellent for all of them. Claire, my interviewer, took me into the office and started asking me questions about leadership and punctuality.

When Claire opened the questionnaire she looked at me askance, as if to say, 'C'mon, mate, are you serious?'

'I know it looks silly, but I can justify each one,' I said.

I blithered on in a self-loving rant that saw Claire pondering what sort of idiot she was interviewing. She locked me in for an observation.

I was to watch a fella called Graham, the owner of the business, at work for the day. He was a man who enjoyed weights. Atop his bulk was a contrasting comic-book character face with fierce blue eyes. Try to imagine Bert Newton's head attached to Andrew Symonds' frame. His hair was falling out but he maintained a 'do of sorts.

Graham was a lunatic. He explained that when we arrived at a shopping centre in Vincent we'd be selling raffle tickets to raise money for a hospital. After setting up he began selling the tickets with an extraordinary intensity, focus and calculation.

He swapped from salesman to mentor, from mentor to accountant, from accountant to boss in a blink. It was bizarre. As I stood witnessing his sales skills, he told me that the key was 'intensity on the inside, indifference on the outside'. It was a statement that made me think of serial killers. Graham stepped aside and allowed me to sell a few tickets. He gave me the job.

I worked with Graham the following day and he outlined the rules of selling. 'Divide the shopping centre into territories,' he said, which made me feel as though I were a Galapagos finch, but I didn't tell Graham that. If you couldn't sell Galapagos finches, Graham wouldn't be interested. Human traffic flow was divided in front of us. I took one side and Graham had the rest. The division was a bench chair, the appointed border of a sales war raging at our table, unbeknown to the passing shoppers. 'Do not pinch each other's customers,' he told me.

When I glanced in the direction of an approaching customer, the intensity on his inside popped out and said 'hello' on the outside. 'Mine, mine, mine,' he'd screech like a four year old in possession of a hotly contested piece of Lego.

Another rule was not to talk to each other's customers. This was the case even when the customer drew you into conversation. Apparently, in order to be a good salesman, you had to suspend all manners and behave like a right bastard. As much as I tried, I couldn't help but engage with Graham's customers. I was met with looks that implied I'd just spent the afternoon pitchforking babies in front of schoolchildren. This man was serious. He'd bark at me under his breath while still engaging with a customer. It was weird.

Graham was particularly fastidious about not eating before he'd taken $500 from the public. He told me that he usually reached that goal about three in the afternoon. It was only then that he went to the toilet or consumed food. I thought this was a bit pointless, but if somebody wants to torture themselves who am I to argue? On that day, Graham was able to squeeze $700 out of the public. I managed to achieve $600, which he told me was awesome. After Graham, this was the highest amount made by the sales team, and it was my first day. I was an animal.

The work was horrible. If somebody approached the table I'd ask them how they were going and see if they were up for purchasing a $100 ticket. As we were mainly selling to people on the pension, hassling them for a hundred bucks was cheeky. If they then asked for a $10 ticket, I'd hit them up for fifteen. The game was about creating awkward social moments where the only way the customer could escape easily was by saying 'yes'. The other option of course was to say 'no', but in that case, the customer would have to suffer the ignominy of looking like a tight-arse. This, apparently, was the job. When I told Graham about my ideas on 'tight-arse cornering,' he dismissed them by declaring, 'You're just asking.'

What a bunch of horseshit, I thought. 'Just asking,' was pushy self-interest. 'Just asking,' was neglecting to show respect for people's circumstances. 'Just asking,' was a piss-weak excuse for poor manners. 'Just asking,' was part of the brainwashing technique he used to convince me that doing what we were doing was okay. Every human instinct said it wasn't. I had to ask myself if this job was worth it. Did I really need to do this in order to continue my hitchhike, make radio and write stories? Yes. That night, I spoke to Laura on the phone and she encouraged me to plough on, knowing I'd need the money. She was right, I did. Her school term was bumbling along with all the regular joys and pains of teaching. Right now, teaching seemed like a great job.

Graham was constantly imparting the message about 'maintaining the mentality'. This was difficult because I kept feeling as if I was hassling and haranguing people. I was abused, insulted, ignored and deplored so it was difficult to keep the vibe upbeat. One of the other key concepts he preached was the suspension of judgement, which really meant that nobody was too poor, old, young, retarded or drunk to buy a ticket. Another of Graham's focuses was keeping it positive, but what I heard in my head was 'keep focused on greed'.

Back in the office, Graham was a unusual creature. Every time a fellow salesperson said something negative, which could be something as simple as 'I can't sell any of these fifties', he'd either ignore them completely, dress them down or change the subject. On one occasion I made the mistake of declaring that it was a quiet day in the shopping centre and that's why I hadn't sold many tickets. That inspired a lecture on the difference between excuses and reasons. I was using excuses and not finding reasons. I was an arsehole, obviously. I felt like declaring him an excuse for a human and putting him through a retraining program that involved kindness and orphans. Lots of orphans who all hated raffles and owned machetes.

Each morning we were put through 'training' lectures. The topic for the morning was often inspired by the mistakes of the day before. The day after my 'excuses' faux pas, the focus was on hardening up through the tough patches. He even drew a graph about it. He was the prince of chump.

One morning Graham broke down society for us. He wrote on the board.

job

work

career

profession

in business

He asked us what we thought a job was. Nearly everyone in the room was thinking, 'This … now … it's a job.' Nobody was game to say it though, because Graham's big blue eyes were pleading for something else.

'A job is like being a garbo,' he told us.

This was going to get weird, I could tell.

'So what's work?' he asked us.

'Working in a newsagent,' somebody said.

'Yes, yes that's it,' he said, all enthused by people getting into the swing of things. 'What about a career?' he said, nodding at me like an aggravated marmot.

I was expected to say teacher. Instead I said, 'Working at Flight Centre.'

As this was not what he'd planned, he just said teacher and kept on going.

I pointed to 'profession' and said, 'It could easily be a profession.'

'No. Doctors and lawyers do professions,' he enlightened us. And there we were, we teachers thinking that we were a profession. Sorry, Graham. It did occur to me to tell him that all of these concepts are subject to individual perception, not his ludicrous concepts of the world. It turned out that the whole point of all this psychobabble was to point at 'business' and solicit the response that businessmen and women get 'respect' and are 'honoured'. Graham told us that through Dunk Sports you could become a person in business and therefore be at the top of society's ladder. That was the big enticer.

On Sunday, my only day off, Graham asked if I could help him move his stuff up to his new flat. I agreed to, knowing that

I'd dodge it as I had a radio show to plan. He probably just saw it as a rite of passage for me to make it to the big time. I saw it as a pain in the arse and a wanton misuse of his status as boss. At two o'clock I received a text from him asking me to give him a call … when I got a chance. I went to bed. I woke to the phone ringing. Surprise, surprise, it was Graham. He tried to load me up with guilt about not helping him move his stuff. I couldn't have given a fuck. I thought he was a prick for trying to steal my only day off.

Later in the week, Graham saw two employees grabbing the wrong equipment. He rolled his eyes in front of the other six sales staff and said, 'Stupid is as stupid does.' That really angered me. He was trying to create a pressure culture in the office. Wasn't it enough to have us fleecing pensioners all day? Did we have to put up with this shit at 7.45 in the morning as well?

After eight days of selling shit I couldn't cope any more and canned it. I waited in the office to tell Graham I was leaving. I asked Sam, another salesperson, if she could wait outside. Graham piped up. 'No Sam, stay here. It's alright; I know you're leaving, John. It's fine.'

Sam had respect and left anyway. Graham had already pre-empted the conversation and was probably very practised at it. I'm not sure if I was meant to be impressed by his sagacity in 'scenario prediction' but I wasn't; I just thought he was rude.

I sat down to have an exit chat, which is a friendly way of parting company. He pre-empted me again and said, 'Don't bother greasing me up, it's unnecessary.'

'Look, Graham, stop trying to control everything. It's annoying. Let me say my piece and I'll move on.'

'Okay. Go on.'

'You're incredible at what you do and I've got a lot of respect for that …'

'Look, as I said, don't grease me up …'

'Graham, just let me say what I want to say.'

'I don't feel you've been honest, John. You didn't do the things that you said you would.'

'What do you expect of a new employee? You've got the power base. Of course we make proclamations of enthusiasm and commitment. We are trying to stay in a job, there is no choice.'

This was followed by scoffing laughs from Graham.

He'd been setting up this moment since our first conversation. He was a hell of a control freak with prepared justifications for nearly every available scenario in selling raffle tickets. My feeling was that Graham had set up his life with minions around him to feed his beliefs. I figured most tunnel-visioned egotistical psychopaths either get rich or kill people for sport. Graham was getting rich. His focus was on the bottom line. Mine wasn't.

At the end of the stoush I told him that taking money from pensioners wasn't fun for me and thus I needed to move on. I also explained that the way he ran his business was like a cult. The look on his face was priceless. On leaving his office I went to shake hands with his indoctrinated young girlfriend, Jane. She looked at me and said that she couldn't, because she didn't want to get into trouble.

'Trouble?'

'With Graham,' she said.

'Jane, you control you. Don't allow yourself to be controlled by him. Christ almighty, be a real human.'

Jane looked in Graham's direction like a panicky rabbit. I scoffed at the absurdity of a relationship like theirs. Sam, the sales girl, who'd walked from the office earlier, shook my hand and wished me well. I left feeling euphoric.

Being in sales was shit and being around an adult bully was even shitter. But what had I done to my goals? I fretted about where my next dollar might come from.

16
Snob

After eight weeks on radio I left Townsville, hopeful that the hours I'd put in to my announcing would leave me with an audition tape that might see me accepted into a broadcasting course at Swinburne University or WAAPA, the Western Australian Academy of Performing Arts. I didn't do any paid work again, ringing mum instead and asking, 'Can I please have two grand?' She said, 'Yes,' and I grinned with pleasure at having had a plan come together.

I hitchhiked inland all day until I got to Charters Towers, where I stayed the night in a caravan park. My sleep twisted and flipped in a series of dreams about failing to get into a broadcasting course at a university. As soon as the sun hinted at possible light, I got up and wandered around the campsite. It was a morning that would turn angry people passive. It wasn't fair to other mornings.

I packed and stood by the Flinders Highway waiting to get a lift further west to Mount Isa. Flies buzzed about me as I stared hopefully at the cars leaving a nearby petrol station. After an hour, I started to think my attempts at radio and writing were stupid and that I wasn't good enough to step away from teaching. Maybe I should just carry on being an educator. It's less invasive, less patronising and probably of greater benefit to society. What was I trying to prove? Who was I trying to be?

Car after car went past. People looked at me incredulously as if I was hell-bent on sodomising animals or breaking the legs of their children. I focused my entire positive power into the situation and got nowhere for three hours.

Then Henry pulled up. He was dressed in a 10-gallon hat and Hard Yakka shirt, like a lot of blokes I'd seen that day. His freckles belonged on a giraffe. He was 44 years old.

'Thanks for picking me up. I've been waiting here for three hours.'

'Three hours? Bugger that! I'm Henry.'

I stayed quiet and observed the car for a moment so as to find something to start a conversation about. I noticed a stock whip.

'Are you good with one of these?' I asked, pointing at it.

'Long as they keep the cows away,' he said. It was easy to forget that stock whips had a real purpose. I only ever saw them on television, when cowboys used them to crack cigarettes out of mouths. Their real purpose was so much more banal. I contemplated telling Henry that, but thought better of it and moved on.

'Nice bush here, Henry,' I commented.

'Okay country, that,' he replied.

Henry seemed a bit reticent. I sensed a man who only talked when he drank, and for that reason I thought he probably drank a lot.

'What are you doing heading this way, mate?' I questioned.

'Going back to Richmond. Got a new job on a cattle station. Me boss gave me till Sunday to grab me stuff and crack some beers.'

The phone rang and he answered it. 'Yeah, Bob. I'm free for a couple of days. Feeling like a beer, for sure.'

I was starting to get the idea I would be the designated driver, which may have been the sole reason for my extraction from the dust. 'Would you like me to drive?' I offered.

He swung his head sideways, opened his eyes wide and nodded. At the next town he grabbed six XXXX Golds and I jumped into the driver's seat. He consumed the first beer in 30 seconds, hurled the empty can out of the window and cracked another one. That caught my attention. I hate littering. I didn't care that he was getting pissed. That was the point of my presence, but cans on the side of the road are an unnecessary eyesore. Still, it was no cause for rebuke. I was in his car, soaking up his generosity. And for all I knew he had a shotgun under the seat. I imagined saying, 'C'mon, Henry. 'Let's turn around and pick that can up.'

'I'll shoot ya, ya fuckhead.'

Henry was a bit of a greenie, which surprised me a bit. He answered lots of questions about his local environment, proclaiming a distaste for introduced species and the poor management of bore water. He pointed out that the scrub between Pentland and Hughenden was not good cattle country.

'Not enough nutrition in that grass,' he told me.

'Oh, right,' I replied, wondering how an animal could survive out here at all. He went on to tell me how he'd harvested wild growing sandalwood for Indonesian incense and that it was worth $2000 a tonne.

'Shit, that's heaps,' I said. 'How much could you fit on a semi?'

'Fuck that, just get it, get heaps of it.'

'Could you crop it? How long does it take to grow to a harvestable level?'

'Four years. It's too fucking long. Can't do that.'

It struck me as a completely viable length of time to wait for $2000 a tonne. Henry had piqued my curiosity, but his abrupt answers didn't inspire further questioning. In our conversations I learnt that he was now sniffing the wind for something better, and I started to form a hypothesis about Henry. He was a short-term thinker. To him, whatever was fun was intrinsically good and everything else could go and get fucked. The theory explained why, at 44 years old, he'd never been married or had kids. But what of the parallels with my own life? Thirty-three, no kids, had a few different girlfriends and wasn't living with my current one. Was Henry me in ten years? Just another, 'Na, fuck that,' man. It was a worry.

After getting back into his LandCruiser at Pentland, Henry leaned towards me and said, 'It's called the Highway of Death, this.'

I looked at him.

'Two hitchhikers got killed. A teacher lady's car broke down and some fellas got her in the bush and raped her. She managed to escape, though.'

'Jesus,' I said.

'A dude recently got bashed to death with hammers and there are two people supposedly buried out in the bush who haven't been found.'

'Fuck, I hope I don't get raped, or bashed with hammers and buried, that'd really ruin the trip!' I said, trying to lighten the mood, but really wishing he'd stop telling me such morbid tales as I had a long way to go yet.

More and more I could see that Henry was a pretty sharp customer, but limited by his own paradigms. (Shit, who was I becoming, my father?) I'd grown up amongst such bushies, blokes who had set their own glass ceilings, sharp as whips but dumb when it came to realising their potential. How do you get a bloke like Henry into a more useful role in society? It seemed like a waste of brain power.

Before we drove into Hughendon, Henry rang someone called Amanda. He didn't even greet her as she answered the phone. Instead he began with, 'Want some meat from the butcher in Hughenden?' This sounded very euphemistic and it took all of my self-control not to interject with a wink, nudge or lewd gesture.

I could hear her talking at the other end.

'I should be right, I reckon,' she said. 'I've got enough for the week.'

'I'll get ya a forty bag. Take it easy. See ya.'

And he hung up.

He asked me to drive to the butcher at Hughenden. I was touched. Henry had picked me up, bought a $40 bag of assorted meats for a lady friend and harped on like an environmentalist for an hour. I was starting to really like him. Then vmmmph, another can out the window. His contradictions were wonderful. I pondered upon my own. I'd worked as a schoolteacher for years, telling children not to drink excessively, yet I was often spied bumbling out of the bottle shop loaded to the hilt. I'd instructed students to live a healthy life and stick to their dreams, only to go home and play Nintendo while eating

Doritos all weekend. Life's weird if contradictions don't exist. Our irrationality can help make us, and the psychological paths to contradictory behaviours are insights into our being. Talking up respect for farmland then lobbing beer cans at it was hilarious.

The town of Richmond appeared on the horizon. 'Ya gonna love Richmond,' said Henry, 'and you can stay at my joint if ya wanna.' I nodded with enthusiasm.

He was right. Richmond looked awesome. It had a lake and loads of happy little kids running around.

When we dropped off the forty bag to Amanda, I scanned her body language for signs of flirting or intimacy with Henry. I could detect nothing. These bushies were harder to read than Tolstoy. We then swung around to the pub. When we walked in, two Aboriginal women touched their faces with the joy of seeing Henry. I sat down with them, Sharnee and Karen. At the same table was a bloke called Joe. They asked about me.

'I'm a science teacher but I gave it the arse so I could hitchhike around the country,' I explained.

'What's a science teacher doing hitchhiking?' Sharnee asked. She'd already picked me as a fake.

'It's fun, I guess.'

Sharnee and Joe were a married couple. Pretty soon their progeny poured through the gate of the beer garden. They were little Aboriginal and white-fella kids, as cute as buttons. The first one looked unhappy, the second one angry and the third one pissed off. One after the other they hit Mum and Dad up for Coke, chips, Burger Rings and Coke again. No, no, no was the clear reply. I talked to the adults for a further twenty minutes before the eldest girl began an earnest attempt to hassle mum into returning home from the pub. I sat there watching and listening.

Joe said to her, 'You're a little bitch, fuck off!'

It came as a surprise to hear a grown man speak to a child like that. I swear like a trooper, but there is no way you should tell a kid to fuck off. I'd had my moment with Borhan, but that was a moment, not a permanency. The way Joe had said it gave me the impression he said things like that all the time. So flippant. The girl continued her hassling and Joe said, 'Go on, fuck off, ya little cunt.'

I stood up thinking I'd flatten the prick. Then I came to my senses and walked away, and went looking for Henry. Joe was a stern reminder to me why it was important to leave teaching. I'd like to cure the issues kids develop from having a father like that, but while teaching science, I'd never be able to.

When I found Henry, I asked him if he needed a lift anywhere because I was going home. He needed to go home too – he was as drunk as he was going to get. When we got back to his joint he asked me if I was going home now. I wasn't sure if he was really asking me to leave or joking around. I was getting tired of his drunkenness so said, 'Look, mate, if you're asking me to go to the caravan park, then I'm happy to go. Is that what you mean?'

He looked up at me, confused.

'Na, naaa, your room,' he said, back-pedalling from whatever he was starting.

I felt a pang of anger. I was pissed off and ready to take whatever Henry might throw at me. I was probably just over-tired and fed up, like a naughty kid at the end of a long day.

I lay down on my torn mattress, thinking of Joe's kids. I had the impression Joe would call them all little cunts, all the time, because of the ease with which it rolled off his tongue. I started to reflect on how this journey's voyeuristic quality was patronising on my part. Was I putting myself in these situations in order to feel better about myself? Reaffirming myself as middle class? Was I just there for a laugh? Was I having a midlife crisis? Was I a snob? These were unanswered questions, but I felt very unlike the Joes of the world. Maybe even more middle class. Arseholes like Joe helped me see righteousness in my own attitudes in a way that I'd struggled to get a hold of in recent times. I thought myself a better man than Joe. I hated that. But if my snobbery could be restricted to hating people who call their own kids cunts, well, I'd be the biggest, proudest fucking snob of all.

Thinking about the characters I'd come across in the last couple of days caused me to remember how difficult it is to apply labels accurately. For example, I am considered to be middle class and Joe and Sharnee working class, which is classically defined by income, location and employment. Respectively, this labelling fitted us like gloves, however they seemed like moot definitions to me and the longer my trip lasted the more I saw just two groups: nice people and not nice people. Joe fitted the latter and Henry fitted the former.

That night, sleeping in Henry's house, I realised what a vulnerable position I was in. I didn't really know Henry well, but I sensed he was a good fella. In order to affirm my safety, I lay in bed and actively went through the things he'd said and done. It caused me to remember something Sharnee had said. 'Fucking Henry, never got a penny. He's always giving stuff away.'

It seemed true enough, considering the forty bag.

I left Henry's place the next morning. When I got to my hitchhiking spot outside Richmond, the sun was beating down hard and it was only 6.45 am. I stood and watched very little traffic go past – only road trains and council vehicles. That was it. Most work vehicles are under instruction not to give lifts to hitchhikers for insurance reasons. I hated that excuse. It reminded me again of just how scared everybody is of everything.

A truck pulled over and I took my position in the cab. Beside me was a man about 40 years old with a 10-centimetre mullet running down the back of his neck. He told me that his name was Mark, which suited him.

Looking out of the truck's windscreen, I scanned the horizon from left to right. Interrupting the endless sky was a Yosemite Sam doll. Mark gave me a quick tour of the cabin: bed, instruments, electric window, speedo, etc. I was as happy as a pig in shit. Then he started on about himself.

I remember this much: Mark had two kids – one he didn't know and one with his current wife, who he'd been with for fifteen years but only married two years ago. Recently, but not permanently, they'd split. She was credited with getting him off drugs. He'd formerly been addicted to speed and had sometimes spent $2000 a week on it. He'd been stabbed thirteen times and broken forty-two bones. One of his stabbings was across the nose and lip. He'd been bitten by a dog right over his mouth. His ex-fiancée fucked his best mate. Mark and his second-best mate ended up bashing his best mate. He'd spent three months in prison after being sentenced to eighteen months for his part in assisting the bashing of his first best mate. On review of the case they deemed it self-defence. He also claimed to have been in *Mad Max Beyond Thunderdome, The Lighthorsemen* and *Gallipoli*. He'd backflipped a quad bike and super-manned a two-wheeler. He honked at camels and once even ran over one. He'd bungee jumped, skydived, rooted hitchhikers, seen a 6-and-a-half metre white pointer. He'd been bitten on the throat by a fox and chased by a pig that had two broken legs.

However, listening to this, all I heard was: 'I have chronic attention deficit disorder, and three hundred conduct disorder symptoms. I am a freaky deeky, antisocial, psychopathic, pathological loon.' I couldn't help but wonder why he needed to tell me all this. It caught me between two worlds: my love of nutters and my hatred of knobs. Unfortunately, he was just a knob with no brassy nuttiness whatsoever. Oh well, at least I had a lift. I tried many times to chat properly, but failed. It was all about him.

Beyond Julia Creek, the landscape began to change. At first there was a dusty little pimple. Then it was a couple of pimples and a ridge line. Soon enough, it was the whole shebang. It was stunningly beautiful. The land was arid with never-ending rocky gullies. I kept thinking of it as a big cake topped with red-rock icing, with a copper-coloured middle and a yellow cake base. After all, we weren't all that far from a massive uranium deposit. I kept staring left and right trying to absorb as much of it as I could. Mark kept telling me things and, interesting as they were, I was busy staring out at the fierce countryside.

I was lost in my own thoughts, while Mark was talking incessantly. Out of the corner of my eye I noticed we were on the wrong side of the road with a four-wheel drive headed right towards us.

'Look out!' I shouted.

Mark looked up and swerved, narrowly missing the vehicle. I could see a look of pure terror on the other driver's face. I'd never seen a four-wheel drive look so small. It was as if every bit of my paltry understanding of physics reared its head all at once. I'd estimated our mass at 60 tonnes and his at 2 tonnes. He'd have been a pancake had I not yelled out. It occurred to me that people often buy four-wheel drives for their safety features, but dusty airbags don't fare well against 60 tonnes. *Pop.*

For the next kilometre Mark tried to digest what had just happened. I tried to make him feel better about his error.

'The four-wheel drive would have snuck through,' I said. 'I reckon there was enough room. Would've missed us, mate. Not a worry.'

'It wouldn't have happened if you hadn't been here,' he replied. Rather than appreciate my *'Look out!'* he blamed me.

I really should have said, 'I wouldn't be here if you hadn't picked me up, you giant egotistical fuck knob,' but the idea of waiting by the road in the same area that contributed to the deaths of Burke and Wills wasn't appealing. However, it still weighed on my conscience and I felt like a wimp.

Mark went further. 'If I'd not been telling *you* a story, it wouldn't have happened.'

Some people spend their whole lives blaming others for everything that happens to them. It's sad when you see it in a

40-year-old man. At what point will a bloke like Mark have an epiphany and realise, 'I made that happen, it was my fault.'? It would have been amazing to hear his testimony in court had he killed the four-wheel driver. 'It was the hitchhiker's fault. He distracted me by listening to my stories.'

I sat there pondering both his and my behaviour. I'd blamed many others during my life: teachers, parents, brothers, sisters, bosses, bullies, cousins, lecturers and anyone who was around. I'd spent a good deal of my existence unmotivated and uninterested, so when something happened that was my fault, I deflected, blamed or used excuses. I was so good at it I could have won an award for it if one existed.

My sister Annie once said to me that I could justify anything. I'm painful to argue against because I've a morphing philosophical base. Keeping it grey allowed me room, made me difficult to pin down. Someone needed to pin me down many years ago, set me straight. People tried, my parents tried, but I was impossible. I dug a nihilistic and existential grave for myself. So far this experience was giving me time to reflect on it and to drive harder out of it. I needed to live the life I'd dreamed of.

Mark dropped me at a caravan park just outside Mount Isa. I watched the blame-truck drive off down the road. After checking in to the caravan park, I settled into giant shed that doubled as the common room and began to watch TV. I couldn't concentrate. My brain started speculating about possible recipes for life success. How do people achieve goals that they really want? I thought about my father, who'd more or less lived life without regret. If he wanted something to happen, he just went and did it, no fuss, no worry, he just got on with it. Laura was much the same, which made me wonder if I was going out with my father. Jesus, this was sickening stuff! Both of them had the ability to stick to the path they'd chosen. How they had managed such assuredness was beyond me. My life was defined by insecurity, theirs wasn't. Perhaps that is why I had opted for Laura as a partner. Maybe my father's assuredness was his most admirable aspect. Just then, a bull ant walked coolly past my foot, no hurry, no worry, and I saw in its walk, something I had not yet achieved for myself.

17
Darwin

Out of Isa, I got a few lifts all the way to Darwin. A normal bloke named Brad dropped me at the house of my friend, Elaina, where I was going to stay with her and her husband.

I spent most of my time in Darwin making audition tapes for radio courses around Australia. Being accepted into one of these courses was vital to my future, a future that I hoped would make me a lot happier. On the first Tuesday of my arrival, I was interviewed on the phone by Paul and James of Swinburne University. The interview began well enough.

'John, whereabouts are you and what are you doing?' asked James.

'I've been up in Darwin for the last few days. I can't leave, my friend's got a pool and air-conditioning. It's all too easy.'

'Oh. We've got some ex-students working at Hot 100 FM in Darwin, have you listened to that?' said Paul.

'No, to be honest. I've been listening to downloads of Russell Brand's radio show. He's brilliant. Do you know him?'

'No.'

Now this struck me as amazing. One of the most talented British comics and radio hosts kicking around, and this radio expert didn't have a clue who he was.

Paul went on. 'Oh you should have a listen to Hot 100 FM. They're good.'

The chance of these guys being anywhere near the standard of Russell Brand was nil. Through flogging his ex-students' work, Paul seemed to be big-noting his course and himself. I'd already applied for the course so it was already sold. It's like signing the deal on a new car and the salesman trying to sell the very same car to you again. *Idiot*, I thought.

The next question was a pearler and threw me into spasms of panic. 'Tell us a story from yesterday in 60 seconds.'

First, remembering yesterday was difficult on any day. Second, everything I thought of was shit.

'Ah, well. Yesterday ... In the afternoon I went to pick up a car at Pickles Auction house. It was the second Toyota Aurion for the couple I've been staying with. Everything in it was stylish and opulent. Which has been the opposite to my current situation. They've got two flash cars and a posh house. I have a backpack and a Shellite cooker. Before I got here a week ago, Elaina was on about getting some nice hand towels for my room. Why she worried about me having hand towels, I wasn't quite sure. I'd been sleeping next to roads eating $1 packet pastas and washing my face in truck-stop bathrooms. I couldn't have given a poo about hand towels, a roof was already awesome enough.'

That was my story. Even halfway through I began kicking myself, which made the story worse as I was distracted in the middle of the delivery. The whole thing was an unquantifiable shit-fuck. At the end, I couldn't judge Paul's response. There were no laughs, just a general petering out of a vibe that had hardly existed in the first place. At the conclusion of the interview I was asked to send in an audition CD. This surprised me, and I assumed they were just being polite.

The following Friday I had a phone interview for WAAPA. I thought I needed extra self-belief, so beforehand I kept repeating, 'I am good enough to do this, I am good enough to do this, I am good enough to do this. I have talent, I have talent, I have talent.' My normal mantras go more like this: 'I am too dumb. Other people know more than me. I'm past it. I'm a wimp. I'm not funny.' I'm constantly at war with my self-doubt. It's a disease, and choosing to go into radio was part of trying to kill it off.

When the phone rang, my heart popped a valve.

'Why radio, John?' asked Jo on the other end.

'I think my skills transfer better into radio than they do live performance. I have a lot of little characters and voices that work very well in the medium of radio.'

'Who told you that?' an interviewer named Dave then asked.

I distinctly remember my eyes going wider. It was a confronting question and a lie was required in my answer.

'I got feedback from other hosts at Triple T (the radio station I'd worked at in Townsville) and some feedback from listeners and friends.' I hoped I sounded convincing; I was lying my tits off. The only person that truly thought the voices worked was me.

They concluded the interview on a very positive note, saying I was definitely up there in the mix and it would be great if I could come and see them in Perth before the month was up. I let out a whoop of joy when I hung up. Country boy did good!

With my interviews behind me I now had to sit tight and hope for the best. Radio … maybe.

On my second Sunday in Darwin, my friend Elaina took me on a surprise tour. Darwin proved to be languidly beautiful, despite the heat's distracting omnipresence. We drove past Gardens Oval, where some young blokes were jogging around in blue jumpers getting ready to play AFL.

'They're going to have a game! Let me out!' I said.

Elaina stopped and I bid her farewell. I watched the blokes warm-up, though the idea of 'warming up' was bizarre considering it was more humid than Ecuador. Ten minutes into the game I'd made up my mind that I would play the next week for the team in blue, the Uni Rats. I looked the team up on a website, found their training times and made a plan to get involved.

The following Tuesday I went to training, a little nervous. It was rudely hot and it felt stupid to be running around in it. Sweat was draining from my eyebrows in a torrent. At the end of the session I was weary but elated to be back on the footy radar. Driving back to Elaina's in her car, I listened to the radio, became bored and got lost in my own thoughts. I'd never really considered why I had taken up football, but I knew that footy clubs allowed me to be me. My boorish sense of humour, natural aggression, need for risk and passion for victory were valued. These 'features' were not appreciated in other circles in quite the same way.

After the next training session I was selected in the firsts to play Tracy Village. I attended on the following Saturday. For the first quarter of the game I remained on the bench, which is a version of purgatory. You sit in between heaven (football) and hell (non-selection in the first eighteen). Watching the game, I could see that I'd have some impact if they'd just let me on the field. It was perfect marking conditions but that wasn't going to last for long. In the distance the clouds were brewing, not like they do in the southern states, but like Beelzebub's rage.

After the first quarter, Coach Shane sent me into the forward pocket. After five minutes the ball headed in my direction and I broke free from my man and took an easy chest mark. I was 50 metres out and had a chance of making the distance if I kicked close to the man on the mark. I put the footy on the ground as if I knew what I was doing and wiped my hands on the grass. I was being a pompous wanker and I loved it. The only thing I didn't do was throw grass in the air to ascertain the wind direction. Off the boot, the ball crashed straight into the man on the mark. Woops.

At about the ten-minute mark of the second quarter, somebody honoured another of my leads with a loopy kick into the forward line. I took fifteen steps, sprang up and marked it. I was about 35 metres out, on a slight angle. I stepped back four paces and stabbed the ball through the goal. The uncomplicated routine worked. If there was a medical test for ego, mine would have blown the machine apart. I high-fived and patted bums for at least half an hour. I was contemplating a lap of honour when the ball was bounced. Away we went again. After the goal, I was stuck with their best defender, a fella similar in skill and physical ability to me, only ten years younger. My arrogance had escalated to such a point that when he and I stood in the square I said to him, 'If the ball gets kicked down you may as well just let me mark it. I'm far too strong for you. I look skinny, but the power is raw!'

He laughed.

I think it'd be harder to dream up a bigger wanker than me. The heavens opened for the second half and every possession after that was terrible. I'd gone from arrogant goal kicker to 'turnover king' in a matter of droplets.

At the end of the game, which we lost by 35 points, I sat panting in the change rooms, staring into space. I was exhausted. Playing three short quarters did me over. My droopy-eyed delirium soon turned to wide-eyed joy as I was handed an ice-cold Melbourne stubby. Despite not knowing a soul at the Uni Rats, I was in the embrace of something familiar, something I loved very deeply. I was at home, safe and happy.

After two weeks in Darwin I packed all my gear up and took off. I sent my audition CD to Swinburne and walked the 2 kilometres from Palmerston to the Stuart Highway, where I hoped I'd be able to cadge a lift to Katherine. I'd only waited five minutes when a bloke called Brett pulled over in a hotted-up Commodore. We chatted animatedly until I worked out he would be taking me only 5 kilometres, at which point I felt deflated.

'How do you go getting lifts around the joint, John?'

'Not too bad. But outside of Mount Isa I waited three hours. Fucking miners don't pick up hitchhikers as a rule.'

'I'm a miner.'

Brett dropped me off about a minute later and I was left standing in the slim shade of a sign while 33 humid degrees raged around me. I felt like a fuckwit – I'd insulted a bloke who was kind enough to pick me up. I stood beside the road, kicking myself, when Brett's Commodore came sidling up to me.

'You're back, Brett. Fucking terrific.'

'Yeah, I got home and thought, I haven't got anything else to do. I'll go and give him a lift out to the edge of town.'

How great is this country when you can insult someone you don't know, they forgive you and then do you a favor all within the space of ten minutes.

A few lifts and many hours later, I was dropped off in the small town of Adelaide River, 115 kilometres south of Darwin. There are 200 human residents, 200,000 flies and one pub. The main street breathed a sticky lethargy. Tired, long-distance motorists stood talking in the shade of gum trees. I was moving in and out of the shade as empty cars went past every twenty minutes or so. At one point a van pulled slowly out of the petrol station and moved towards me. It had to, because I'd positioned myself in a must-look-at-me spot. The approaching van was full of dreadlocks, tie dye and hippy pretense. I was excited, thinking they were practically obliged to pick me up, for the sake of Gaia, Mother Earth, Bob Marley, Marcus Garvey, Ben Harper, Tim Flannery, Bob Brown and peace on all the earth. My dead certainty, however, turned into just dead. They all made a stern effort to look in the opposite direction and accelerated past me. When I used to hitchhike back in the early nineties, only one hippy in ten would drive past. I had to question what the modern-day hippy was all about. Nowadays, it appears that dreadlocks are not underpinned by anything except dirt.

18
Warping

After the Borhan incident, I survived at Stanford High School for another four weeks. There was plenty of other work around and I was happy to take it.

In March I caught up with some mates I'd made during a trip to Portugal, fellow Aussies Adam and Troy, who now lived in London. I wasn't a huge fan of going down to London from Manchester because I felt adopted by the north. Proper northerners hate London. Nevertheless, I was very much looking forward to catching up with Adam and Troy because their company meant things would happen. They were special units.

My mates lived in Brixton, which may as well have been called Shitston, Crapston or Arsehole-of-the-earth-ston. Within thirty seconds of my arrival at the Brixton tube station I'd been offered speed, uppers, downers, benders, crack and pot. It wasn't the most convivial atmosphere, and needless to say I was concerned for my safety. Adam met me with a welcoming and enthusiastic holler, which I happily soaked in. He seemed relaxed in this ghetto and that put me at ease. Adam was always bouncing off the walls, a shining light of positivism in all environments. It was contagious and I found myself inadvertently mimicking his style.

We grabbed some cans of Tennet's beer and rocked up at Adam and Troy's tiny flat. To call the flat a shoebox would be implying it was small. It was smaller. They'd partitioned the room in half so that one side was Troy's and one Adam's. Troy threw himself on me when I walked through the door, hugging me like a madman. We exchanged excited stories about who we'd been rooting (I was single again) and any unfortunate pub scuffles we'd been involved in. Laughter was crashing against walls, rebounding into my ears in a positive feedback cycle.

The three of us then took off to a party full of Finnish people. Loads of blondes were in the room. Opaque blue eyes bobbed around like racquet balls in a swimming pool. It was a master race. Sam, Adam's mate, asked if I wanted some ecstasy. The idea simmered in my mind. I'd never had it before. 'How much?' I enquired. 'Nothin''. For all these years I'd been watching my mates sniff coke and speed, drop Es and eat LSD. I wasn't sure whether I wanted to be the one pointing up at the sky exclaiming, 'There's a dragon!' Much less the dude hugging street bums saying, 'I love you.'

I'd been a pious saint in comparison to my pals. However the recent split with my girlfriend had caused my mind to break a fraction and the idea of giving it a chemical holiday was appealing. My self-control fell away and I ate down the tablet, immediately feeling that pang of fear you get dipping your toe in the unknown. After half an hour of zero intoxicating sensations, I became worried that I was immune, but relieved I wasn't dribbling in an emergency ward.

Oh well it was free, no bother, I thought as I smashed back another can.

Then my belly warmed; something was changing. An involuntary smile waded across my face and the drug was taking control of me with a kindly euphoria. My beer tasted like drips of sunlight and my face beamed. My mate Adam was smiling at me as I'd told him it was my first time.

'What d'ya reckon?' he asked.

'It's fucking magic, why has it taken so long for me to drop this shit?'

Everyone seemed rapt that I was off my guts. Oh, what a sense of achievement when one converts another to their sin. People always do it. Come on, take a drink, have a shot, try a bong, blah blah blah. It seems to be a process of sin validation.

Share the sin and it lessens your own, especially if you're converting a long-term abstainer. I guess if I could convert people to sucking themselves off with vacuum cleaners, I might feel better about doing it to myself in the first place.

I was still slamming down cans with gay abandon, having a terrific time. I slipped in a little kiss with a mildly overweight Finnish girl. The E had wiped away my discretionary ability and I wanted to boil in sexual intercourse. I was seeking it, but no real opportunities were offering themselves. The E was beginning to wear off so it was time to find the dealer. Sam was kissing a belter in the corner and on my arrival, he handed over another E and simply winked.

It appeared that drug people didn't need words.

I was soon spiralling in bliss again. The party was winding down. It was four in the morning and there were no sheilas left. I went looking around the house. Each door I opened had different sexual positions on display.

'Sorry …' I murmured each time, feeling like a pervert.

I sat on the lounge room floor watching the feeble light of dawn come through the window. I was protected by a fortress of empty beer cans. It was a little heaven. My mind was dog-paddling in happy days. It was easy to drift back to my childhood, when I was swimming in the creek at Greendale, jumping out of the willow tree and bombing my brothers, 32 degrees of sunshine smashing on my back as I warmed my body in the grass. I fell asleep with my smile pressing into the carpet. In the morning – or it must have been lunch time – the boys woke me. A blanket was lying next to my face, couch cushions were propped on my body and I was using a Tennet's can for a pillow. Drugs, eh! I felt vacuous, confused, ill, cold and thirsty. Errraarruhggh.

'We're going to the pub,' Adam said. It wasn't an invitation, it was a demand, and one I welcomed.

Walking out into the drizzle helped my head. Hangovers are easier when wet. I ordered a first pint of Guinness. Two pints in and the laughs began again. Those blokes had been all over the world, wreaking havoc. It was tremendous to hang around with kindred proverbials. Adam told us about his father, who he said was an overbearing cockhead. Because of this, when Adam turned fifteen he took off to live in a caravan on the border of the Simpson Desert. Lizards and beer were his friends, he told us. I told him about pissing on the blue tongue.

Sam was fossicking about in his coat pocket and I knew he had something devious in mind. He pulled out his bag of chemical magic. He offered the bag around and several people took a pill. No doubt, I was keen, however I needed to get back to Manchester that night so I should've just caught a bus home. But temptation was rolling its bright light in front of me and I opted for the E. I'd gone from abstainer to addict in twelve hours.

The day rolled into the night and punters came and went. We annihilated our minds. When I woke up in the morning my tongue was glued to the roof of my mouth. Sleep lined my cheek bones like salt drying onto a beach towel. Staggering to the Tube, I jumped on the Central line and passed Cockfosters, grinning. I arrived at Victoria station and loaded up for Manchester. The first hour of the bus ride was effortless as the grog was still doing its job inside me, but after its effect wore off, I rolled into depression and sadness. Without a doubt, it became the worst trip of my life. Pain surfaced in self-recriminating thoughts … *Why did I reject my girlfriend? Look what it has done to me. Why am I living here? Why am I such a weak man?* I couldn't help but think of people who had peace in their hearts, kindness in their minds and forgiveness in their nature. All of the things I did tended to be hedonistic and ultimately negative. It was a mystery to me how anybody ended up mentally stable in any way, shape or form. How would I find my equilibrium? Clearly drugs were fun but they weren't the answer.

The bus rolled and bumped its way down the M6. I was teaching the following day and that unsettled me. I'd been a teacher for a year and a half and I was already dreading going back to school. I was becoming aware that I'd backed the wrong horse, but still I understood that teaching was better than reading water metres. I mulled over how friends had suggested I try stand-up comedy in the Iguana bar down the road from where I lived. Yet the thought of it filled me with such unparalleled fear that I was only able to muster defensive laughs. They could see the real me better than I could.

I was back at work on Tuesday teaching kids who were better soccer players than me how to kick the ball.

19
Kids

It's 2006, England is behind me and the months have ticked by without too much incident. In fact, I'm relatively fit and happy. I'm bopping about madly hosting pub trivia and generally having fun. However, one thing irks me and I can't quite let it go. It's my work. It was shit in England and now it doesn't feel all that good here either. It's the fact that nobody seems to care that Australian secondary schools are not the best places to be. Adults are stressed and children are battling with little support. It frustrates me immensely.

I arrive at school for another day. The big yellow orb is sending down jets of the warm stuff. Kids file past me. I listen to the sounds of the hallway. 'Fuck you.' 'You're fat.' 'You fucked Dylan, didn't you?'

The unpleasantness is phenomenal. I listen for a kind word but that world is silent. The driving negativity of adolescence shatters egos and creates gods.

I stick my foot out and trip a kid I know. I just raise my eyebrows when he looks at me. He feigns to punch me. I smile and he moves on.

It's getting near the end of the year. Kids smell relaxation. They sniff it in October and drink it up from then. It's December.

I sit my Year 9 class down in front of me and I ask them to open up to page 56 of their textbook. I'm watching Jason. He is chewing the ear of some poor kid. Every kid is sick of Jason. My eyes are boring holes into the flesh on his face but he cannot feel it. My skin bristles and the class goes deadly quiet. No page turning … nothing. I get up close to Jason's ear and scream, *Jason, open your book!*

Yelling is not what I normally do. Most of my students know this, but when students don't change or become aware of what is around them, *boom!* I explode.

I start to lecture Jason sarcastically. 'Well, Jason, what a surprise that you're ignoring others around you. So unlike you. Normally, you're always thinking of others. I'm in shock. You're the least selfish fellow I know. Chances are you'll be off soon to India to help the poor and starving, a nice young man like you. Bet you can't even handle sitting in the classroom. You just want to get out there and help old people cross the street with their shopping.' The class laughs at him. He looks at me, his mind saying, *I hate that prick, I hate that prick, I hate that prick.*

My mind is no different. What a wonderful world it is. But at the same time I hate it when I lose control and deliver vitriol.

I stop winding myself up and get on with teaching the workings of a synoptic chart. I set a pop test at the end of the lesson. It's a hard one and the best mark in the class is six out of ten. Some days, seeing the levels of motivation in children is like dying of a slow bleed. I start my ineffective lecture on motivation but 'Blah, blah, blah,' is all they hear.

If only they knew my own levels of spurious motivation they would understand that I was a hypocrite. Thank God they don't know me. I must leave this job, it makes me sad.

By that time I'd had enough teaching experience in Australia to feel the heartbreak of the job. I'd begun to understand the flaws in the public system and the role secondary schools played in capitalism: we looked after children while their parents made money. I felt that a different societal system would have better outcomes for young people. What that system was, I didn't know. I knew fundamentally that the money and hours poured into Australian schools were not gaining great outcomes. The public school I worked in was a good one, yet the number of kids coming out of it to enter tertiary education was well below what I thought to be satisfactory. After our Year 12 students graduated, I'd ask which ones qualified for law and medicine. The answer was always one, two or none. It wasn't good enough.

I'm not going to blame my colleagues, because there were some brilliant teachers at our school. The gun teachers could engage a classroom of the toughest students with incredible will and commitment. Others were softer and moulded the youth around their brightly burning positivity. Then there were those who used humour, guile and leadership to draw the youth into their fold. I revered these teachers, but never saw myself as one of them. I tried hard, but felt fraudulent, like a lot of beginning teachers. In my school there were also a few lazy, system-bleeding individuals. Some teachers would run straight to a line of waiting students upon arrival at the school and leave at 3.30 pm as if the institution was on fire. The same ones would often moan about the rates of pay. Career teachers (and I realise the necessity of this) would set themselves up with year 7, 11 and 12 classes so as to avoid the staunch anti-educationalists of the middle years. Some had the temerity to turn their nose up at the teachers who slogged it out with the more difficult classes, as if they were super teachers. Some hadn't taught a middle-year class in a decade. Teaching for thirty or forty years is a marathon effort. Trying to avoid classes that cause frustration is a sensible choice. So I couldn't really take them to task about any of these things. What's more, I didn't yet have the confidence to confront people about their manoeuvring.

I could see the state pouring money into the system, but it was the attitudes that were coming from home that were the real problem. At least 50 per cent of students didn't respect education and the opportunities it could afford them. They did, however, respect the artistic process, proven by the perfect cocks, boobs and vaginas covering the desks. I'd ponder how to change a societal attitude to education. Sometimes our best students were migrants from a poor country who could see the opportunities a good education could provide. Our worst were the ones who saw a manual labour future; they would seek to waste everybody's time as a source of entertainment. The mechanisms for punishment were weak and the students' parents self-righteous. I wanted so much more for our students, but didn't have the skills to deliver.

20
Drought

From Adelaide River I got a lift with a Zimbabwean all the way to Katherine. After a restless night sleeping outdoors on a picnic table with insects crawling across my face, I dragged myself back to a road. By seven, I'd walked a kilometre in the boiling sun and popped myself in the shade of a tree. One hour elapsed with not even the slightest sign of a possible lift. I tried to focus on thoughts of my previous day's successful hitchhike, thinking it would help.

In the second hour I put on my iPod, listening to a Russell Brand podcast, then threw rocks at signs. In the third hour I recognised the cars that had been past previously. I figured it must have been a free day at the tip because cars kept going past loaded with household crap and smiles. Getting rid of an old blender must be like shedding a skin.

The rest of the traffic offered a mix of friendly smiles and waves and sarcastic smiles and waves. I found them equally infuriating and difficult to distinguish. The lines were blurring. I was muttering obscenities at every passing vehicle. The power of positive thought could lick its own arse. My head was turning dark. I was flying off the handle, kicking stones and punching nothing.

'Faark!' I yelled into the swelter. 'Bastards!'

This went on for twenty minutes. I hated myself. I hated them.

The fourth hour went on in much the same way, except for one moment of brief optimism when a road train pulled over and parked on the grass. No lift. One car even had the temerity to honk their horn and wave. This caused me to promise to the heavens that I would track down every last member of their family and bash them to death with a honky horn. I trembled. I breathed. I tried to centre myself. I got to wondering how my father ever coped with long waits by the side of the road. How did he hitchhike halfway around the world without pulling signs out of the ground and beating motorists to death? Maybe he had, but he surely wouldn't share a story like that. Dad's thirst for adventure was infectious and he'd passed some of it down to his children. His stories about Iranian homosexuals getting in his bed and Brazilian police officers sticking guns in his face enthralled us when we were younger. But the only thing sticking in my face now was searing beams of sunlight and I was getting cranky.

By the fifth hour I'd turned to throwing rocks again and attempting to read. A distraction would help. I was reading *Man Drought*, which I had given as a gift to my dad last Christmas with the full knowledge that I'd read it myself. Essentially, I had bought Dad a gift for me. My dad was correct in that the book wasn't good. I did, however, learn a little about myself. It informed me that I was in the last year of being in the really-eligible-bachelor phase of my life and moving into the grab-and-marry phase. That brought out all my insecurities and damned me to further reading. One of the chapters was about generation Y sponging from their parents. I'd recently borrowed $2000 from mine and intended to live in their house when I returned. Although I was generation X, I was acting like Y.

I continued reading to learn that Baby Boomers had worked hard for their money and had lived life with the attitude, 'You get what you earn.' I'd managed the opposite to them: 'I deserve it all.' I fitted the authors' opinion of my generation. I'd travelled, had fun, been to uni and saved nothing. I was an ill-equipped, discipline-less twat. I felt shit and swore that I would knuckle down to real life upon my journey's end. Maybe I could work in an abattoir slitting cows' throats until I retired at seventy, as a penance for my wasteful youth. I could be a good citizen, lose my dreaminess and settle down to being a man. I snapped myself out of my daydream by yelling, 'Ah, ha ... fuck you, shit author! No fucking way!'

A roadside cane toad looked mystified. Without the slightest sense of irony, I threw rocks at it.

It must have been 42 degrees. The sixth hour came and I broke my junior record of waiting six hours and five minutes for a lift. I was desperate to get moving. The thought of another night sleeping on a bench with ants crawling all over my face didn't thrill me. I couldn't work out what to do.

The driver of the truck that had parked on the grass came out of an adjacent building and needed help with a bale of hay. I assisted and he asked, 'Where are you off to?'

'Anywhere that way,' I said, pointing to the horizon.

'I'll be leaving in half an hour if you want a lift, mate.'

The drought had broken.

Three hours down the road I was dropped at Victoria River, which was surrounded by escarpments and scratchy vegetation. Everywhere I looked the rock was the same rusty red as the dust that makes up the Red Centre. After setting up my tent at the rear of the pub, I took off towards the sunset for a walk. I wandered past the windows of the pub, where the bushies craned their necks to see what I was doing. I walked along a road at the edge of a river valley. Eons of wet seasons had carved out a wide riverflat, with channels that functioned as overflows for the river during the rains. The scale was enormous. I imagined crocodiles skulking down the channels and snatching the cattle I could see among the trees. The road was pulsating heat like a stove top. Sweat was running down my inner thighs. When I got to the top of an escarpment, I sat staring at the Victoria River. It could have been 50,000 years ago.

Later I strolled into the pub, where road construction workers were having a beer. The pub was decorated with typical paraphernalia of the outback: pictures of floods, boats and sunsets. I sipped on a Melbourne stubby and stared at things. Everyone sat in a mutually understood silence, in recognition of the fact that it was nice to have company but words wouldn't necessarily add to the experience. *Air Crash Investigations* was on the telly and they were re-enacting the pilots in trouble. I thought about how people enjoyed this kind of thing. How I enjoyed it. It's the same plot every time: happy travellers board a plane, plane takes off, everything is going smoothly then plane crashes in forest, everyone is dead, the black box confirms that the plane crashed for a reason. End of show. Never a joke. No-one cares. Change the channel to *Seinfeld* …

Not long after that, I dived into my sleeping bag and slept soundly.

I awoke at 5.30 am. The flies were already about and the sun wasn't even up yet. I packed and stood by the road with a freshly made 'Kununurra' sign. Two hours. A van stopped.

Ulrich and Isabelle were a recently married French couple who touched each other a lot. It felt weird considering for the last couple of weeks I'd been surrounded by lonely blokes who said mental things. I enjoyed the difference. Isabelle asked me questions and my answers were put through a lengthy interpretation for Ulrich, who spoke very little English, before they responded. We went on like this for hours. It was testing, but they were too lovely to suggest an adjournment.

At about midday, Ulrich mistakenly drove 20 kilometres in the wrong direction. For me there would have been a fight in a mistake like that. When they realised, however, Isabelle simply leaned over and gave Ulrich a kiss on the cheek. At that point I had to wonder if this was an indicator of the great qualities of French culture or simply two people in love. In the end I decided Isabelle had heat stroke.

I sat on the floor of the van for hours, using my Kununurra sign as a cushion. At one stage I shifted a metre back and noticed I'd imprinted Kununurra on the floor. It was in permanent black ink. Shit. I worried about it for 200 kilometres. When we pulled up in the evening to camp, the Kununurra stamp was still there on the floor. I showed it to Isabelle. She didn't seem angry.

'It will come off, I reckon,' I said.

'With a bit of soap,' Isabelle said.

'Yes, yes probably,' I stated, knowing it wouldn't. I felt so guilty, but I didn't have enough money to give them any. I loved these two, especially Isabelle who was sweet, generous and forgiving. She had even started to worry about whether I'd get to my WAAPA interview on time, bless.

Our roadside camp was somewhere between Kununurra and Halls Creek, right on the edge of the Kimberly. I looked out at ridges lining up on the horizon like precursors to much wilder country beyond. With the sun setting it looked magnificent. Unfortunately, to ruin my bliss, the smell of a dead animal floated in, all carcassy, from somewhere in the bush. I sat down in the darkness and tried to listen to my iPod but the smell was too forceful. Standing up, I walked out to the road to put some distance between me and it. I strolled past another camper who was pottering about his caravan. Since our arrival at 5 pm the camper had been drinking stubbies and singing out of tune to eighties rock songs. It was not difficult to see him as a serial killer because all the factors added up perfectly: alone, pissed, big and he was building a fire. Very bad news indeed.

We hadn't recognised each other's existence until an exchange as I walked past. 'What'd ya reckon? Get some diesel in that shitter and set the fucking thing alight?' he asked, referring to one of the nearby long-drop toilets. I couldn't help but notice the lack of conversational preliminaries before cranking out a sentence like that. He was clearly mental, but at least I now knew what the smell was.

I blurted back in surprise, 'Oh, sounds like a good idea.'

I kept walking towards the road, past the toilet. I'd covered about 100 metres when I heard a voice behind me.

'Yeah, real smelly!'

I spun around to find that he'd followed me up the track. 'Stinks,' I said to the darkness as calmly as I could.

I could only just make him out 30 metres away. He was sitting on a jerry can of diesel next to the loo. Obviously his expectation was that I would help him set fire to the shit in the toilet.

'That torch would be fucking handy,' he said, noticing what I had in my hand.

I backtracked and shone my torch into the loo for him.

'Faarkin' stinks,' he observed.

'Sure does.' No point in arguing the obvious, especially with a mental.

Together we poured diesel down the loo. I wasn't to know the perfect amount for such an occasion but he poured at least 10 litres in. I wondered if that was a bit much as he pushed me out of the way while dropping a bit of lit toilet paper in.

Wwvvmpphh! Western Australia lost half its oxygen at that very moment. It was sucked down the toilet, making the most awesome sound I'd ever heard. Who'd have thought burning shit could make such a fun noise? For a moment I worried we were going to burn down the whole toilet block by the way it lit up the night. I stood back and enjoyed the moment, pissing myself laughing. I slapped my thighs, roaring hilarity into the heavens. I gurgled, snorted, twisted and contorted. It was fucking ace. It took me a full minute to stop. Poo burner then introduced himself as Gavin.

'Shit, that's fucking hilarious,' I clamoured.

'Yeah, I could tell ya fuckin' thought that. It's killed the smell off.'

I'd had this happen before, laughing when nobody else was. Watching people was my hobby and if I saw something that didn't fit the norm I was tickled pink. Gavin didn't fit the norm at all.

Gavin was as friendly as could be, just uncouth. We meandered back to his campsite and chatted about burning excrement and the fuel economy of four-wheel drives.

I thanked Gavin for the laugh then went back to my camping spot and lay down on top of my sleeping bag. Looking upwards at the widest, brightest night sky available on Earth, I thought how wonderful it was that Australia owned Gavin. Imagine how boring life would be without him.

The next morning I woke to a friarbird hopping around my head. It was the size of a willy wagtail, with brown feathers and stern eyes. I sat up, letting out a yawn. The friarbird skipped backwards in shock. Gaining courage it came back, tapping at my food bag. I shooed it away, tickled by its cheek.

I made coffee and forgot about the bird, until I heard a claw on synthetic material. I swivelled around to witness it hopping around inside my tent, pecking at things. I was amused, but as soon as I stood up to deal with the situation the bird started evacuating its arse like a broken sewer pipe and shat all over the shorts I was intending to wear that day. Not amusing. I got the bird out but it was too late – the tent was whitewashed.

The Frenchies called me over and we got going towards our next destination, Broome. After two hours of driving through sparse bush I was excited to see roadworks coming up. As we got closer, I saw a guy sitting in a deckchair under a picnic umbrella. He was an enormous Maori. He had a stop–go sign resting against his deckchair as if to say, 'I don't care if you stop or go. Do whatever.' I started laughing. On his head was a broad-brimmed hat. Dangling from the brim was fly netting that covered his face. Sweeping down from the fly netting were two white leads that were attached to a PlayStation Portable. His feet were propped up on an esky and he had a can in his hand.

I was pointing and laughing, 'Look, look, the laziest Maori bloke ever … Better than a burning toilet.'

Isabelle laughed loudly and nudged Ulrich. Ulrich looked over at him and giggled as if to say *'No wonder it was so easy to sink the Rainbow Warrior'*. That was the last highlight before the journey became uneventful. Except for a scrub fire.

Arriving in a Broome caravan park, we all got drunk together. The beer took hold and I began vocalising my worries about my WAPPA interview. It must have been very boring to Isabelle and Ulrich, and I'm amazed they both didn't run into the sea hoping for the loving embrace of a box jellyfish.

21
Weasel

My hangover suffused every pore of my skin, every blood vessel, every brain cell. Broome's heat made it worse. My mind skipped from topic to topic and I couldn't make sense of anything. I sat in the Kimberley Klub, the backpackers, all day, unable to do anything useful. I retired early.

The next morning I grabbed my laptop and took up a position in the open-air lounge of the backpackers, where I typed and typed and typed. My writing was rambling, but it stopped me going stir crazy. Writing had that effect. My sedentary state allowed me to observe the run of the joint. I'd sussed out lovers' tiffs, protective boyfriends, slutty girls, prudish celibates, young lovers, macho wankers, gamers, cup-of-tea addicts, four-day-old hamburger devourers, constant eaters, kind old travellers, egotistical middle managers and out-and-out dickheads, just to name a fifth of what I witnessed in the thirteen hours I spent in front of the computer. I even saw a guy with a smiley face emoticon tattooed on his back. I could hardly believe it.

The most charming moment of the day came when a friendly German fellow called Janic asked, 'You are very busy typing – are you writing an article? Are you a journalist?'

'Ah … well, sadly it's a no on both counts there mate,' I said, wishing I was able to tell him that I was writing a story for *The New Yorker* magazine. Instead, I told him that I was writing about pooing next to Irish Dave's foot when I was in Townsville. Janic's inquiry did, however, make me think about my ambition. Journalism is lovely stuff, but every time I'd tried to write on a serious topic I infused anecdotes about wanking, pooing or farting. They always seem relevant. As I read over the Dave story, I kept wondering who on Earth would ever read this self-indulgent drivel. It was all me, me, me. I liked writing the stories down, but I hated what it said about me.

By the time I'd stopped typing late in the afternoon, I'd obtained a raging beer thirst. So I quenched it. At the bar I sat next to a fella who had been walking around shirtless all day, trying to attract women. We started chatting and I found out he was a hitchhiker. We immediately started talking,

'So where are you from, Andy?' I asked.

'Belgium,' he replied.

'Where have you hitchhiked to in Australia?'

'Once from Melbourne to Darwin, once from Perth to Sydney and ...'

I interrupted. 'Holy fuck, you're accomplished!'

'It's easy and it's free. Why not?'

'Yeah, it can be easy, but I waited six and a half hours for a lift the other day. What's the longest you've waited?'

'One and a half hours.'

I wondered why he was so much better than me. What was I doing wrong? I began to assess possible answers. I was much taller than him, and I was older. I looked more aggressive. My dress sense was crap compared to his soft European garb. It was then that I realised my upturned collar might have caused longer waits. I looked more like a jock than a wistful drifter. People had been asking me if I was a PE teacher for years and that's exactly where I was fucking up my dress sense. I needed to hippify. I asked myself, *Could I wear a feathered hat, a shell necklace, tie-dye and dirty clothes?* No, I'd prefer to wait an extra five hours for every lift.

I needed to reconsider the fact that I'd been proclaiming how good I was at hitchhiking to anybody who would listen. I now knew I was in the low to super-fucking-shit hitchhiker range.

I asked Andy, 'So ... what do you do for sleeping and all that jazz?'

'I kip in my sleeping bag on the side of the road.'

'What, no tent?'

'No tent.'

'What about a mat? Do you sleep on a mat?'

'No.'

'So hang on, what if it rains? Do you get wet?'

'I get wet.'

'Holy fuck. That's awesome.'

Andy and I went to a local pub and drank more. It was an evening most notable for being punctuated by uninformed dickwits. At one stage, Andy started talking to a group of girls who were beauty therapists. They were pompous beyond belief, and their pomp was matched only by their ignorance. Cuticle was the biggest word they knew. I got bored very quickly of squeezing a conversation from girls who laughed not at jokes but at moments they thought would humiliate the closest male. I mentioned to Andy that we needed to talk to other people because I was likely to start giving these sheilas too much shit and get kicked out. Instead, we nipped off home to the backpackers. Andy went to bed and I was left talking to the bloke with the emoticon tattoo. I'd previously assessed him as a knobhead, and such sober thoughts can unfortunately turn into drunken words. Mr Emoticon started rambling on about how amazing travelling was, which annoyed me, so I contested every point he made, simply to amuse myself. I was managing to keep a lid on any real cheek until he said to me, 'Look mate, you're being malevolent.'

'I'm not,' I retorted, though I probably was.

'You don't even know what it means,' he said.

'Does it mean that you're insulting me by assuming ignorance?'

Inside my mind I was giggling like a girl. When I get a knob to take the bait, it's bliss. I hoped it would all end in anger and confusion. 'Do you think it is similar to bellicosity?' I asked. 'No, hang on, maybe it's closer to vindictive tyranny or belligerence. Or do you believe I have pugnacious intent?'

'Oh, then,' he said. 'Perhaps you do know and you're intelligent,' he told me.

This was a definite case of him trying to pull back. I was pretty sure he was gay and good luck to him, but his gayness added a quality to his bitchiness a heterosexual fella had no chance of attaining. This made things even more fun, so I thought I'd up the ante a little.

'I'm sorry, mate. I'm not intelligent, but I think I've detected that you're a thief.'

'What? No fucking way! Why would you say something like that?'

'You've a thiefy look to you. Thief.'

'Oh my God, you're so rude. I'm not a thief.'

'I think you are. I could tell you wanted to steal my laptop today.'

'My God, you're intolerable.'

'You've got small eyes. It's usually a sign.'

'A sign. What the fuck do you mean?'

'A sign of a weasel thief.'

I'd gone past the point of no return. I knew I had to get up and leave before he sprayed me with mace from his handbag.

'*You are sooo rude*. You don't know what you're saying, do you?'

I was on my feet now. 'Come on mate. You're a happy guy, don't get so angry.'

'Yes, I am happy, but you're an arsehole.'

'Yes, I believe you are happy because you've got a fucking smiley-face emoticon tattooed on your back. Good night, weasel thief. Try not to rob me or tattoo LOL on yourself tonight.'

I let out a cacophony of guffaws that'd rival a flock of cockies and left. I couldn't have scripted more fun, but I was out and out turning into the greatest arsehole on earth. I went to bed. I'm pretty sure he'd still be bitching about me now.

The next morning it was time for me to leave the Kimberley Klub. When I woke up I groaned at the thought of myself. I am such a fuckwit. I'd have to walk downstairs and potentially run into the poor fella I'd wound up for my own amusement. Sometimes I'm the type of person I hate the most. I was locked in a paradox. If anybody else had been behaving like I was towards the Emoticon guy, I probably would have stood up for the poor bastard. I wondered why I needed so much drama. Is life without it boring? When was I going to engineer the sort of drama that meant something, rather than this sort of frivolous shit? I'd been doing stupid stuff like that for years, and it always made me laugh in the moment, but grieve in the future. Was it too late for me to change? It felt like something worth thinking about, so that I might maturely deal with an emoticon tattoo in the future. Or not.

Luckily, I didn't run into him. I walked out to the edge of town.

I needed a lift soon because I was required in Perth for an interview with WAAPA. I waited in the diminutive shade of the Derby sign for an hour before a four-wheel drive, dual-cab ute pulled over to give me a lift.

The cab was relatively opulent. It had air-conditioning, which beat wedging myself in the shade of perpendicular roadside signs; music, which thrashed silence; and a seat, which flogged sitting on my *Lonely Planet* guide.

Joe, the driver, had spiky blond hair with the merest hint of a mullet, a square jaw and a lively, handsome face. His left eye squinted a bit and he bore a small amount of facial growth. He was shirtless, which showed off his multiple tattoos — a wolf, a Yin Yang symbol and Celtic patterns. His muscles were locked into his bones and he had large arms, a thick torso, finger saveloys and a strong forehead.

He looked to be my height.

'So, where are you going, mate?' he asked.

'South,' I said.

Laughing, he replied, 'I'm going to Perth if ya wanna go that far south.'

I then had the quandary of deciding whether to hit Perth quickly with Joe or slowly with other rides. WAAPA was 2000 kilometres away.

'Fuck, yeah, that'd be great,' I said. I'd signed a contract without having a clue what I'd got myself into. But that's what this journey was all about.

Joe mentioned that we'd be heading through a place called Meekatharra, which I assumed was somewhere on the Western Australian coast, but I wasn't sure and began to freak out. I looked in my *Lonely Planet* guide and found that Meekatharra was inland, on the Great Northern Highway rather than the North-West Coastal Highway, the one I'd intended travelling on. I'd committed to a desert trip. The idea of travelling the West's interior appealed to me, but I didn't have the foggiest idea what might be there. I envisaged a long drive through nothing.

My contemplation was unsettling the car vibes, so I began a discourse. 'What are you doing back in Perth, Joe?'

'I live there, mate. I'm fucking *going home!*' he yelled.

'So what were you doing up here?'

'I fix specialty engines and do tricky mechanical jobs. I'm a fitter and turner. I've done heaps of different shit, though. Built trailers, driven trucks, worked seventeen years on mine sites.'

'Shit, money good in the mines?'

'At one stage I was on four grand a week.'

On money like that, this bloke should be loaded. But Joe had 'wild man' written all over him and they don't save. Drugs, alcohol, hookers, cars and fluffy dice are spending priorities. I guess I wasn't all that different, but I had less money.

'I'd fuckin' spend cash hand over fist,' Joe went on. 'I used to have a Statesman HQ with fuckin' beautiful chrome rims. Every fuckin' nut on it was chromed. It was fuckin' perfect.'

I'd never dream of spending dough on chroming. He probably should've practised aerosol chroming instead. It's cheaper.

By now I was sensing Joe was a fairly aggressive bloke but I wasn't getting a frightening vibe off him.

'You like cars and trucks and all that sort of shit then?' I asked him.

'Used to drive prime movers there for a few years.'

'I like trucks,' I told him, feeling quite idiotic as soon as the words had left my mouth. He looked at me quizzically. I felt I owed him an explanation.

'If I ever got rich I'd buy a Kenworth or a Mack truck and just use it as my run-around vehicle,' I explained. 'Pull up at work looking all cool. Be awesome, I reckon.'

'That's fucking stupid,' said Joe.

I was beginning to understand that Joe wasn't a sensitive type. He was right, however. I'd tried to relate to a road-train driver by implying that trucks were a fashion accessory. I changed the topic.

'It's good to be in a state that's pretty strictly AFL. Do you support the West Coast, Joe?'

'Na, I'm not into that shit. I like boxing. I've done a lot of competitive boxing.'

That's not what you want to hear from a bloke of a similar height and weight with tattoos and a booming voice. For most of my lifts I'd estimated that I could've overpowered somebody who was enthusiastic to assault me. Not that any were, but it was a comforting thought. If Joe was interested, I'd be bashed. It was clear that he wanted to be considered the alpha male as we travelled the highway towards Port Hedland. He was loud, direct and swore profusely. He banged the back of his hand into my arm when he was making a point, just to let me know who was boss. I was not motivated to enter the competition and displayed subtly submissive gestures in order to let him know. I needed to seem weaker, yet still a man. In order to convince him I was not a homosexual wannabe truck driver, which he clearly didn't want me to be, I told him a story about giving Joe Righetti heaps of dead arms in Year 10 maths.

'What, when you were a fucking teacher?'

'No, a student.'

'Jesus fucking Christ.'

I was pretty hungover on account of staying up late drinking and calling people weasel thieves. I sat in silence more than I normally would have. Joe took this as a cue to crank up the CD player with a four-CD set called 'Rock Hits'. It featured Lynyrd Skynyrd, White Snake, Alice Cooper, AC/DC and others. It was really 'Cock Rock Hits', but I didn't want to argue. Joe revelled in the tunes but wasn't a foot tapper or a head banger. I'm pretty sure he would have thought that 'gay'. The source of the noise was giant wood-lined speakers on the back seat of the dual cab. They looked out of place. He informed me that he'd had to install his house speakers, because the vehicle's normal speakers were 'tinnie piss-ant shit ones'.

Joe cranked the music up loud, but kept turning it down to say, 'You don't mind the music do you, mate?'

Even though the music was too loud and a bit awful, his good manners inspired me to continually answer, 'Shit no. Crank it up.'

As a result, my ears were filled with the poignant angst of double-necked guitar at full volume. It was easy to imagine Joe dreaming he was a lead guitarist in leather pants with his cock rubbing against the back of his 'axe' and his hair flowing wildly in the breath of 60,000 stadium fans.

I was still being quiet by my standards but Joe wasn't to know that. He must have been contemplating my state of mind, though, because the next thing he did was to drop a pile of pornographic magazines on my lap. Normally, I'd be whooping it up, overjoyed, but at that moment I was melancholy. I kept dwelling on the sort of dickhead I'd become and the aimless life I'd chosen. I wanted to break out of it with intellectual stimulation. I wanted to read something that didn't make me feel like a loser or give me an erection. I needed a broadsheet newspaper – a certainty for keeping me flaccid. I wondered if it was a test of my heterosexuality, after all I'd said fuck-all about my girlfriend, Laura.

'Oh, ta,' I said and started leafing through the porn.

I continued to flick through a magazine for a while then put it down. I stared out the window. I noticed Joe look over, confused by the fact I hadn't picked up the next one, so I picked up another magazine and leafed through it. But this time, the boobs and vaginas had a slight, mood-shifting effect. I took a bit more interest in the shape of nipples and the curve of hips. My heterosexuality was returning, but I was still craving something with substance. I put the magazine down again. This time Joe couldn't stand it and said, 'Had enough already, mate?!'

'Can you ever get enough?' I replied.

I reluctantly picked up another one and flicked through one of the filthiest pornographic magazines I'd ever seen. I knew I was being bullied, but it was better than getting my head flushed down a toilet. The content of the magazine caused a perk-up in interest. Now I was having the opposite problem. How long was it acceptable to stare at scenes of bondage?

Joe asked me to drive for a while, so I did. If I didn't take the handbrake off after attempting to let out the clutch he'd say, 'Handbrake'. Or if I didn't stop the wipers, 'Wipers'. Quite oddly, it wasn't annoying. He only said stuff when it was warranted. For a ruffian, Joe was exceptionally safety-conscious.

As the afternoon continued we travelled through Port Hedland. The town sat next to the ocean on the edge of the desert, and I'd expected a bit more. It was a mess of shipping containers, railway lines, smoke stacks, truck parts, old cars, ramshackle accommodation and barred-up windows. If industry was a person and that person did a shit, Port Hedland was that shit. Things picked up for us, however, particularly for Joe, because he bought a case of beer from a bottle shop on the outskirts of town. *Oh fuck, here we go again*, I thought. *Another Henry-from-Richmond situation.*

We made our way out towards South Hedland and then turned towards Newman and the West's vast interior. It was bizarre to be heading into the desert, but I loved that we were covering all this ground. WAAPA didn't feel so far away all of a sudden.

It wasn't long before the terrain became unexpectedly interesting. Huge boulders sat in piles all over the undulating wilderness. As the sun went down the vastness and isolation dominated. Pink hues speared purple clouds and red rock bled through soil. The little undulations gave way to sweeping ridges, peppered with vegetation that survived temperatures over 30°C every day of the year. Small hills cast shadows that never ended. Thunderheads appeared in the distance and forked lightning swirled through black clouds. It was a truly fantastical experience. Unknowingly, I was travelling through the Pilbara. I'd known about it for years, but the directional change in my hitchhike confused me. Joe never mentioned the Pilbara, but I hadn't given him cause. Still, I wondered if he knew the area's title. It was a beautiful, drawn-out sunset in a unique landscape. In celebration of the beauty of the environment, Joe threw an empty out the window. He really was like Henry.

I carried on the conversation. 'So, you like car racing, you were saying earlier?'

'When I was a young fella,' Joe said, 'I loved the drags 'n' shit. I'd buy two fuckin' sets of tyres every weekend. I'd blow both of 'em pulling rollbacks at the wharves in Darwin.'

To me, rollbacks were the withdrawal of a former government's policy and I felt that would be difficult for Joe to achieve on a wharf in Darwin.

'What's a rollback, Joe?'

He looked at me as if I'd asked what a pencil was. 'Fucking hell, mate. It's where you put the car in reverse, roll backwards, slam it into first and drop the clutch. The tyres smoke up beautiful.'

'Sounds like fun.'

'Yeah. All good until things fuck up, though. One of me mates once pulled a rollback on the wharf and ended up in Darwin Harbour. He went to prison for a year because of it.'

'Prison. He must have done more than that?'

'Fucking oath he did.' I let that one go through to the keeper without inquiring further. Not sure I really wanted to know anyway. And besides, I was still perplexed over the car sinking. I could never understand that mentality. I've lived a lot of my life without much money so being wasteful and sinking a car off a wharf confused me.

'But did you go to actual drags?'

'Yeah, I used to work at 'em as well. I was a cooler.' He looked at me to see if I recognised the term. I didn't. He was probably thinking I was the dumbest person he'd ever met. 'Ya know what one is?'

'No.'

'It's a guy who's paid to step in on fights. You just get right in the middle and break 'em up.'

'Shit. Did you earn much dough?'

'Yeah, $250 a night.'

'How'd you do it?'

'Blokes would punch me in the jaw and I'd take the punch and say, "You really want to do this?" That usually did the job.'

I'd earnt money in many ways, but never by getting punched in the face. Even if I'd wanted to be punched in the face for a living, I wouldn't have known how to get the job, I'd never seen the position advertised at Centrelink. I told Joe about my fight with Phil and he responded in a way that suggested I should take up baking. I was trying to relate to him on his level, but it was like an astronaut discussing space travel with a taxi driver, so big was the gulf between our histories. But that's exactly what made him interesting to me. Talking about rollbacks and coolers beat discussing the curriculum and yard duty, hands down. It would have tickled me pink to introduce Joe to the staff at my school. Although, over the years, I think most of the staff had taught many Joes.

We continued to drive as the sun left the sky and stars started to appear in their thousands. Joe had finished about fifteen beers and was happily consuming more, 'Fucking hitchhiking, hey?' he mused. 'Fuck, I could never do what you're doing. Just standing there waitin' would do me fuckin' head in. I'd get too fuckin' angry.'

'It gets annoying, but I don't get too angry,' I said.

'I get angry real fast. Had to do an anger management course once.'

This worried me a bit. We were about as remote as you can get in Australia, and I was talking to a half-drunk fella about his anger management issues. It got worse.

'Why?' I dared to ask.

'Knocked a copper out. It was an accident, but.'

'How's that?'

'I was fighting two blokes on a footpath. One bloke was in front of me and I was laying into him, the other was somewhere behind me. I felt some lug jump on my back so I threw a punch over my shoulder and knocked out a copper.'

'So what did the judge say?'

'He fucking knew it was an accident. If he didn't, I'd have gone to the can for five years.'

I decided I would never leap on to Joe, under any circumstances. He asked me if it was easy to get lifts.

'Sort of,' I replied. 'Different people pick me up, like some Frenchies who gave me a lift to Broome. But it's funny with the backpackers, because they'll pick you up if they haven't watched *Wolf Creek*. If they have, they just drive straight past. It's ridiculous how they let fiction govern their decision-making process.'

He was laughing at my predicament while winding down the window to throw out another stubby. 'Yeah, it could get fucking worrying, hey? Especially with all the fucking loonies around out here.'

'Oh, na. I don't stress.'

At the time of this conversation I was driving the car, Joe had lapped up twenty beers and it was dark outside. The nature of the conversation turned the air tense, sort of like a slow build-up to my murder. Joe was cackling away when he reached across suddenly and grabbed me by the throat. It was disconcerting, but I didn't bother looking in his direction. I just kept driving. If he was serious he'd have been choking me harder … I hoped. If it was a joke, it was a frightening one.

'Ha ha, ya dumb bastard. Fuckin' got ya.'

'Ya didn't, ya fucker. No worries here, mate.' I was concerned at my situation. Was this the beginning of a head fuck that was to last hundreds of kilometres? Was it the start of a real threat? Was it just a short-term joke and I could soon relax?

He grabbed a stubby out of the esky then reached across and rubbed it against my inner thigh. I instinctively pushed it away and looked up. 'Get out of it, ya poofta,' I said.

This caused him to laugh really madly. He reached across with his hand and gave my thigh a rub. I let him do it so as to give the impression that his bullshit wouldn't bother me. He was making the kind of edgy jokes you only make with your best mates. He was playing on the lack of familiarity between us to try to brain-bash me into believing he was a gay psychopath. I refused to let it work.

'Ya love that, don't ya?'

'Yeah, it feels great, Joe. Keep going.'

At this he really erupted. Laughs poured out of him like a subwoofer in stitches. Arsehole.

It was still really warm outside and we kept stopping so he could piss out all the beer he'd drunk. The stars were dominating. The Milky Way was defined and satellites whipped through the night sky.

'It's fucking beautiful, hey, John?' said Joe.

'I can't get enough of this sort of thing,' I said.

He was standing on the road, spinning in a circle as he pissed and talked.

'What are you spinning for, Joe?'

'Ain't you ever done a piss ring?'

'No.'

'You piss in a ring then the next day the sun bakes it up all perfect. This one'll be here for weeks.'

As soon as he'd finished urinating, Joe began adjusting the spotlights on his ute.

'Is that the right spot for you, John? You're driving, they've gotta be just right.'

His personality contradictions made Joe entertaining. How he could cop punches as a cooler then be so concerned about the spotlights being in just the right position cracked me up. We hopped in the car and got on the move.

'Belt,' he said.

As we drove further and further I came to realise Joe was many things. He was a plucky bloke, a big drinker, a reformed brawler, funny, adventurous, mad and generally a decent sort of a fella.

'I'm gonna sit out the window,' he stated.

'Go for it.'

He wound down the window and did exactly that.

'Woo hoo!' he cried out into the night.

The wind was warm and it was one o'clock in the morning. Joe popped back in after five minutes and said, 'Ya gotta have a go at that, it's brilliant. Pull over, ya cunt, we'll get you out there.'

I didn't want to rock the boat and I really wanted to do it, but I had to consider how many beers he'd had. As far as I could tell, he didn't appear completely hammered.

I pulled over onto the gravel and we swapped seats. I was now perched happily in the passenger window. The warm breeze felt good as we moved off. I leaned back and swooned at the moving stars as I sped through the desert.

'Yee haa!' This was the shit. It was exactly why I liked hitchhiking. *You ... fucking beauty.*

I dropped back into the car and Joe explained that I needed to wedge my legs in behind the seat a bit better so it was safer. He was calculating risks again. *What a softie*, I thought.

At the next piss stop we swapped drivers. By this time, Joe had had twenty-six beers. Ten minutes later, I looked across at the passenger seat but Joe wasn't there. I panicked for a second before realising where he'd gone.

The roof. I was travelling at 120 kilometres an hour. I shook my head. He was one hell of a game unit. When he came back in, I felt a sense of déjà vu.

'You gotta have a go at that,' he said. 'It's fucking awesome. Ya just wedge yourself into the ladder. I sat up for a bit 'n' all.'

The idea of sitting on the roof of the vehicle was immediately appealing. But the same quandary presented itself, and now he'd had twenty-eight beers. Everything else was the same … anger management, violent history and general unpredictability. Still, I relented.

'Yeah, alright. I'll have a crack,' I said.

I pulled the ute over and hopped on the roof. Joe drove off in a sensible manner but it didn't mitigate my fear. I was still hanging on tighter than a cripple to a crutch on a mountain pass. I began hollering at the sky. Unlike Joe, I refused to climb back in the window while the vehicle was hurtling along. One slip-up would've been fatal. I banged on the roof to get him to stop. He braked in a way that suggested he wouldn't have minded seeing me flop movie-esque onto the windscreen.

We settled down after that. The conversation turned to girlfriends and kids. I told Joe about my past and Laura. Joe was very happy with his current partner – he was going to marry her.

We drove through the night. The sun was already up when I

saw a road sign, 'Perth 550'. It was a relief to see a sign like that. It felt as if Perth and my interview with WAAPA were just around the corner. The only problem was that neither of us had managed much sleep at all. We were completely ruined. I'd spent a good amount of my time behind the wheel that night pinching my leg and slapping my face.

I pulled over and drank two cans of Pepsi one after the other, to absolutely no effect.

On the previous evening, Joe had offered me a room for the night on our arrival in Perth. He'd brought it up with his missus, who was reluctant. Joe said this was 'shithouse'. Their phone fight raged until it was declared that I'd probably have to stay in a backpackers.

When Joe dropped me off in Perth, I thanked him profusely for what I felt was an escapade. Society hadn't existed for a while. As it turned out, that would not be the last time I would hear from Joe.

22
Failure

It's 2008, and lately it's been difficult to find happiness. Some days I stand in front of the mirror and stare at my pointed nose. I look more like my uncle every day. I look at the small hairs coming from my nostrils and the dark areas under my eyes. I am not good looking, but I'm not ugly. I'm just … there. My greying hair sticks out from my head, consistently unmanageable. It's curly and wiry.

'Dunny brush.'

'Young Einstein.'

'Gollywog.'

'Get a job, hippy.'

'Scourer.'

Nowadays it's slightly receding, but I couldn't ascribe a rate to it. There is nothing to indicate the speed of the process except for observations of my relations' heads. I wonder if they ever pay attention to me checking out their bald spots then asking their age at every family function. I'd prefer to know exactly the velocity at which it is disappearing, but no-one knows, no-one can tell you. Lately, though, I care less. Some days I look at my head and laugh just because I'm looking at my head.

It's not only my head that bothers me. Often I take my top off to check the flab distribution. I realise that I need a crisis to drop a few kilograms, an event to give me an excuse for a bender where I forget food exists. I can feel small hips, like that of a fattening teenage girl. It's disturbing because I hate fat. It's a sign that I've lost control, lost power over myself.

A year previously I had applied to be on *Big Brother*. I had always believed I belonged on the telly or radio. It's a sickness of the masses that we all think we should be stars. I want some form of notoriety, make no bones about it.

I thought that getting onto *Big Brother* might also help me achieve my dream of becoming a radio announcer. I made my audition MPEG movie on a Sunday. It had dancing and singing and snippets of footage from work. I declared myself the leading local applicant. I called myself a 'local personality' just for a laugh.

Three seconds of my dance made it to national TV in the *Big Brother* advert – finally a taste of the limelight! My students thought it was fantastic and it was a constant topic of conversation for me. To progress to the next level of interviews, I needed to get lots of hits on the *Big Brother* website. Each day I'd check to see how many I'd had. From the beginning, I was in the Top 100 in Australia. I could see a glimmer of hope at the end of the reality TV tunnel. Unrealistic-as-fuck hope, but hope nevertheless, that this could lead me away from my trapped existence as a teacher.

When they culled the bottom fifty through popular vote, I remained in the top half which guaranteed me an interview by *Big Brother* executives. With two days to go before a group interview, I contracted a vicious flu. It crept up on me like a stalking cat, then pow! It hung around for two weeks. On the day of the group interview I was still in the midst of a fever. Rocking up to the temporary *Big Bro* headquarters in a Melbourne hotel had me tingling with nerves. Weirdly, most people looked pretty average. I thought I'd be surrounded by hot glamour pusses. Only a couple of people really stood out, but most of them were attention-seeking plonkers, just like me. I wondered if that was how I was actually perceived on the day. It is strange to be in a room full of bold-faced fame cravers. During the interview process I tried to be honest about my quest.

The attention-seeking aspect was bizarre. Some people chose to stick their necks out so far, I swear they'd begun to look like tortoises. It occurred to me to do the same, but I just stuck mine out the regulation amount.

I was well received by the executives and was singled out for a separate interview away from the others. On my way home I felt that I was walking in the shoes of a potential F-grade celebrity. It felt like I'd done the job to put me through to the next level.

This proved wrong. The next email never came and I remained another forgotten applicant. Fucking great! I could tick off another 'nearly' in my life. That's what I needed, more close calls to lift my confidence.

My next move was to pursue something I'd always wanted to try: stand-up comedy. This felt very bold. The comic lounge in North Melbourne had an open mike night for wannabe stand-up comics, so I went along and gave it a bash. My first routine lasted about three minutes and rolled along the lines of, 'How shit's this … I rock up to do stand-up for the first time in front of an audience of stand-ups. Seems hard. It's like asking a six-year-old boy armed with a water pistol and sunscreen to go and kill the Taliban.' Lame, but it got a quasi-laugh.

Then I moved on to my 'plop-plop' routine: 'When you're in a car with your mates and one of them asks if he can do a shit at the next service station you say, "Yeah mate" and just drive past. This causes a great deal of consternation and remarks. "What the fuck are you doin'? You missed it!" I always look across and say, "Plop, plop."

"Are you fucking kidding me?' my imaginary mate says.

"Do you need a piss as well?' I asked.

"Obviously mate, who doesn't piss a bit when they shit?'

"Plop, plop, pisss!'

"You're rotten.'

"Plop, plop, plop, plop. Wanna hear a song I made up? It's called rapper plop. Rapper plop, plop, whickety-whack, plop, plop. You need a shit, plop, plop. But I won't stop."'

And then I roared with laughter. You can see the sort of quality I'm capable of. Clearly it was awful but, amazingly, for a first go it was well received.

When I went back for a second go the following week, I was already a superstar in my head so I decided being less rehearsed would be a good idea. I leapt up onto the stage and did a slow forward roll and claimed that I'd overdosed on Pepsi Max and it was making me act like a fuckwit. For which I was sorry … zero laughs. *Oh fuck*, I thought to myself.

Then I launched into a two-minute story about how my dog Gus did a shit on the staff-room floor at my school. I imitated his actions and described each shit he did in detail. If I could have reached out into the air I would have felt the vibration of people feeling sorry for me. The quieter it got (and it was very fucking quiet), the louder I impersonated Gus. I did his pre-shit face, and then his squat and shit face as well. I did his post-shit routine where he blissed out up against a window. All that could be heard after the punch lines was the eerie buzz of the microphone.

At this learning night for comedians, the process was that when you finished your routine, the audience analysed your performance. It was hard to draw a lot of positives from the criticism. One fella asked me, 'Do you think you swear too much? Maybe you could use other swear words?'

'What? Like cunt?' I accused. I directed this question towards the questioner with the sort of rage not often associated with comedic evenings. One man in the audience absolutely cracked up laughing and I jumped off the stage and had to stop myself running out the door. I never went back.

Then there's the writing gaff. I've loved reading and telling stories for many years, but it was only around this time that particular revelations inspired me to sit around typing for weeks on end. In my family there are quality writers, including my mum, who has been published, and my brothers and sisters. But when they were performing well in English, I found staring at a keyboard about as interesting as playing with gravel. My sisters especially seemed to have infinite patience for reading and writing, but I just wanted straight-up gratification. They could sit and read all day without needing to rush outside and time themselves doing a lap of the house. And my younger sister's poems were fantastic. She seemed to be able to project herself into a midlife crisis despite the fact that she was eleven.

My first-ever writing focused around roughness and magic. I came up with the idea of writing a story about a water-meter reader who could commune with dogs. They spoke to him with a rich English accent, like most fantasy animals. It was a shit story.

I wrote my second story while I was at the airport in Genoa. I was so bored that I conjured a story about rough stevedores at the Melbourne docks. Born to fight and fuck – stuff like that. I read it to my travelling mate who said, 'Ah, yeah, not bad.' That was something, at least. And while overseas I'd write emails about my adventures. I'd tell stories of the Gaelic football team I played for, that had their first training session after their third match, or nearly getting bashed by a member of the mafia whom I purposefully shouldered in a nightclub. I enjoyed the return emails.

The next stage in my journey was to write a draft of a novel. Losing myself in fantasy was pure joy. I found a space in which I was ultimately comfortable and free to express my whimsy. My mum said it was good, but what else could she say? All of these failures were my first real efforts to change my world into one I wanted. I was happier having a go and failing than repressing my dreams. Something I wish I'd learnt when I was a younger man.

23
Audition

I hoofed off to the backpackers in the centre of Perth and rang Peter from WAAPA. He didn't answer his phone. I'd travelled a long way to have someone not answer their phone. It concerned me, so I jumped on the internet and emailed him.

'Dear Peter ... blah blah ... contact ... appreciated ... looking forward, etc.' My phone rang soon after that and Peter requested my presence on Monday, which gave me a full day of doing bugger all in Perth. Perth's a nice, neat and safe city. I didn't have to loathe traffic or suck in tonnes of carbon monoxide. Instead, I could bumble about the streets looking at beautiful people with a sense of ease.

On the morning of my interview I was nervous. On the way to WAAPA I tried to push the anxiety aside by imagining the lives of the people who lived in the houses my bus was passing. It looked as if they were living charmed lives with their perfect gardens, vibrant roses, shiny cars and smiles. Maybe not, though. Could they be bickering about TV channels, last bits of milk, hair in the basin and who fed the dog? It didn't matter. I wanted to change my life. I wanted to get into WAAPA. I wanted it. I wanted it badly.

Arriving at the university, I entered Building 6 with trepidation. This was going to be pressurised. I walked up a staircase and a fattish, balding bloke appeared at the top. He looked at me quizzically and said, 'John?' I could only assume that this was Peter.

'Peter?' I returned.

'Dave,' he said. I'd happened upon my first error.

'Come through and sit down, mate.'

He took me in to an office where I was introduced to Peter and Jo. To help me relax, they asked how I was going and inquired about my travels. I was quick to confess that I was hitchhiking around Australia. I'm not sure why I felt the need to put it out there. It's like saying, 'I'm a nutcase.'

It got worse.

I wanted to come across as interesting, so I told them about Joe. Drinking, fighting, getting arrested, drink driving – all of it. All they heard was: this man cavorts with criminals. I couldn't stop my self-destruction. Again.

They dropped me into the course-related questions, trying to pull me up before I admitted to 'bashing Lebos' in the Cronulla riots.

'Now, John, we're not quite sure what you think you're going to get out of the course. It's quite a serious course and everything you've shown us so far is about laughs.'

'I thought that was my best avenue to get here,' I said. 'I'm focused on getting into radio as a sort of comical idiot. So that's how I've presented myself to you. I know you're concerned that I'm incapable of serious journalism, but I believe I can produce it.'

Dave piped up in an acerbic tone. 'John, I think you're naive. In your audition, you spoke of having a show that could be edgy and outspoken. Radio doesn't work like that.'

'I was stating my dream when I said that,' I replied. 'I'm aware that it's a hell of a climb to get into that position.'

'It's more likely, John, that you might end up in production or some other area of radio. How would you feel about that?'

'Obviously I wouldn't be as happy as I would be if I could wrangle myself onto the airwaves, but one opportunity leads to another.'

'I've just got a lot of concerns about it, John. I'm not at all sure this course is right for you.'

What the fuck is? I thought. *This is a radio and TV course and I've made my enthusiasm fairly clear.*

Then Peter chimed in. 'John, in the course you'd be required to work with a lot of other individuals in a team. It can be difficult when you're a bit older and a lot less talented. How would you feel about that?'

I was pretty sure that just saying 'ace' wouldn't get me a gig in the course, so I waffled on about trying to learn from them, being competitive and having a go. I bored myself with my answer. But what else did I have?

Jo threw the next one out there. 'John, this course is highly vocational, as we've told you before. It's full-on pressure. We'd be at you all the time, deconstructing you and your ego to turn you into a product. How would you cope with that?'

'I'm up for it. I'm aware that it needs to happen. You're the experts and I'm tough enough to cope with it. I'll take a deep breath when it's required, no problem at all.'

David chipped in. 'I'm not sure you'd be able to cope with it, John.'

'What can I do but assure you that I'm willing to take the hits. I can and I will if you give me the opportunity.'

They put me through an audition process, reading autocues, scripts, adverts and news. I laughed before I did the finance bulletin. Everything else was normal.

Then it was back into the interview room to assess my effort. David was quick to query whether I could take the course seriously because I'd muffed up the finance news. I explained that it was a nervous error and I wasn't happy about it. He made a 'hmph' sound. I was a little taken aback. Everything this fella was projecting was negativity. He had a sort of bashable head on him, and I wanted to bash it. Peter was fine, Jo was reasonable, but David was overplaying the devil's advocate.

When I left the office I felt I'd won over Peter and Jo, but I was sure that David would be arguing seriously against me. They promised to let me know by the end of business that day.

The next six hours turned into an anxious waiting game. I couldn't hold a conversation for more than a minute and I couldn't stand still. I walked in circles around Perth, drank a Guinness and twitched. I considered hanging around and waiting for the outcome at the backpackers. It felt like a waste of time. I needed to be occupied, so I started packing my gear in order to hit the thumb circuit. I caught two buses to get to the edge of Perth. By the time I was on the second bus it was 5.20 pm and still nothing. Then the call came through. It was Peter.

'Look, John, I'm sorry to inform you that you didn't get in.'

My heart sank into my stomach and my eyes iced over. 'Oh, right.'

'John, we debated your case for 45 minutes and decided it wasn't the right course for you. From a personal level, I tried my best to get your case up. I think you've got something to offer. You have a warm, accessible Australian manner, but I just couldn't get you there. I know you're going to hurt, feel horrible and all that sort of thing, but in this case, John, you've missed out.'

'It's okay, Peter, life is meant to test us. I knew if I was to get in it would've been out of left field. I guess I was a bit too far on the left. I'll keep turning rocks over trying to make it happen. Life rolls on.' I'd centred myself with clichés.

The conversation ran for another couple of minutes in this manner. I liked Peter. He seemed like a nice granddad sort of character.

When I hung up, the sadness rolled in and I stared distantly out the window at the woody scrubland littered with grass trees. The bus driver stopped at a petrol station on the edge of Perth and wished me all the best. I'd told him as I'd hopped on the bus that I was hitching to Melbourne. His good wishes made me want to hug him; instead, I shook his hand and stepped off. I was the one who needed a hug.

I rang all the relevant people and told them of my failure. Laura was shocked, my sister Mary was disappointed and my mum was very sad for me. I managed by sticking my thumb out at the passing traffic.

I must have looked like the saddest man on earth. I felt destined to be a teacher till the day I died.

Divine intervention caused a white Holden ute to stop. I peeled back the tarp at the rear and lobbed my gear in.

Aaron was a youngish biochemistry student at Edith Cowan University. He was amiable, but I couldn't listen to him properly as I was still in shock. Instead, I expelled my grief in a barrage of bitter words, full of self-pity. When he dropped me off I'm sure he was laughing about picking up the most self-obsessed idiot this side of the black stump.

I stood on a rise in a town called Bakers Hill, and stared through the passing traffic.

My phone rang. 'John, ya cunt. How you going?'

'Joe! Fucking awesome. How you doing?' I don't know why I said 'fucking awesome'. I guess in painful moments you overplay the brave face.

'Good, mate. Just thought I'd invite ya over. You can come and stay in the shed. Me missus is alright with it. Ride me fucking motorbike round 'n' that. Piss off down Margaret River if ya want.'

'I've already left, mate.'

'Already? Well fucking come back. How far outa town are ya? I'll come n' get ya.'

'I'm gone, Joe. I'm in Bakers Hill and out of here.'

'Faark. Did ya get in your course?'

'Missed out.'

'Cunts.'

'Yeah.'

'Look after yourself, John. You're welcome anytime.'

'Same if ya nip over to Victoria, mate.'

'Cheers mate, see ya.'

'See ya.'

I reckon that speaks for itself and it still gives me fuzzies. I had to love Joe, reformed lunatic that he was.

After a night in a caravan park and another half a day's hitching, I was nearing the edge of the Nullarbor.

24
Stanley

Tom, my next lift, was 55 to 60 years old. Deeply ingrained, sun-bashed wrinkles carved gullies through his face. I figured he was about 5 feet 10 inches. His sun-mottled hand (minus a finger) was lounging comfortably on the steering wheel, his face turned rapidly towards me when he spoke. He had a full head of greying hair with just a hint of a mud-flap. His eye movement was fast and his speech even faster. His body language was trying to send the impression that he was a bit crazy, that he shouldn't be fucked with. That is a common scenario in rides. It's a macho fifteen-minute window in which the driver indicates that you're on his turf and any aggression will be met with more.

Tom's warning was expressed in a bizarre story. 'There are a lot of rough people in Norseman, but I don't give a fuck,' he began.

'Fair enough,' I told him.

'I was at a fucking hole in the wall a coupla fuckin' weeks ago and two little cunts are fucking loiterin' over to me left. I fucking knew they was gonna do somethin'. I could just fuckin' tell. One comes forward and he's got a foot-long iron bar in his hand. I just squared my body up to the little cunt and told him that I'd stab him in the fucking eyes. Right in the fucking eyes. I had a fuckin' Stanley knife in me pocket, see. So I took that out and showed it to him. I couldn't see his face, but I knew who the little cunt was. No problems. He fucking took off. Right in the fucking eyes, I said. Right in the fucking eyes.'

I thought to mention to Tom how wonderfully versatile I considered Stanley knives to be, with a retractable blade allowing for different cutting depths. So if he should come across somebody with bigger eyes, he'd simply slide more blade out for a deeper eye gash. I didn't mention it for some reason though, perhaps I was distracted by a fly.

Five minutes into the ride, Tom began discussing his profession. He'd been a truck driver for the last twenty years, covering the full gamut of runs throughout Australia. 'Later tonight I'll be off to Madura,' he said. 'Leave at two in the morning. You can tag along if ya want.'

I'd found myself in another situation where I'd only just met a bloke and he was offering me a long lift, 500-plus kilometres, where he would drop me off near the South Australian border.

I needed to make a quick decision. My pause must have been too long because he said, 'It's up to you, mate. No worries either way.'

'That would be awesome,' I replied without further hesitation.

'Well, what we'll do is lob around to my donga, stop there for an hour or so then head down the pub for a coupla beers. Sound alright?'

'Brilliant.' I said, happy that I knew 'my donga' meant Tom's miner's accommodation and not his penis.

By the time we arrived at Tom's place, he'd endeared himself to me. The donga was lacklustre, to say the least. There were three dusty, uncarpeted rooms that were littered with bits of mechanical clutter. On the bench outside the front door was an instruction manual and parts for a LandCruiser chassis.

'So what's all this gear for then, Tom?'

'I'm doing up another old LandCruiser. I bought it for two grand from me old mate Jimmy up the road there.'

I strolled over to the manual and read the open page. Paragraphs and drawings littered the page like schizophrenic diagrammatical vomit.

'Holy fuck. How do you make heads or tails of all this shit?' I asked, baffled.

'Been doing it for years, John. It fucking comes after a bit.'

'I could be doing this for years and still not work out how to pump the tyre up. You must have some head on ya.'

'Na, left school in Grade 3. No brains whatsoever. Can't read.'

I paused for a moment to soak in his statement. 'What? You mean to say that you can't read and you can still work all this shit out?'

'Yeah. The diagrams are all I need.'

'Jesus.'

I kept my finger on the page he was on and flicked through the manual. It looked about as simple as chaos theory.

'Jesus,' I said, repeating myself out of pure flabbergast. 'You're a fucking genius!'

'Na, it's just what I know.'

Tom was being completely humble. As a schoolteacher I was impressed. As a human, more so.

As much as I wanted to delve into this anomaly of the human condition, it wasn't my place. But, by fuck I was captivated. It spoke volumes to me about what people will and can do when you take away one option. Tom and I went to the pub and knocked back a few drinks. We returned to Tom's place, at about 9 pm and I went to bed. Not feeling quite like nodding off, I rolled out my bedding and walked off into the bush to talk to Laura on the phone. It was nice to have Laura.

'Hey, sweetness, how you doing?' I asked.

'Good. You?'

'Fucking awesome. I'm in Norseman. That rhymed. Fuck, I'm amazing. You should see it. I'm staying outside this dude's house and getting a ride with him early in the morning.'

'You'll be back sooner than you know it.'

'You should see it here, babe. The stars are ridiculous. They're tinkling, twinkling and doing all that star shit. I've had eight beers and now I'm gonna sleep under the stars. It's going to be awesome.'

I blithered on to Laura like this for ages. I'd had such a good run to get to where I was that I was over the moon. It was beyond fantastic to have made such great ground so soon. Although WAAPA still pained me, the eight beers in my belly allowed me to forget about it while I drifted off to sleep.

I was woken by Tom. 'We're going now, John.'

'Ah … right, hang on. No worries.' I jumped to my feet and looked at the time. It was 2.30 am. I staggered through the hours of that early morning into Tom's truck and we moved out onto the Nullarbor.

The Nullarbor Plain stretches across 1200 kilometres of Western and South Australia. Saltbush, red dust, bluebush flick by in equal proportions for hours and hours and hours. Tom dropped me at Madura as promised and after linking truck rides that were organised by him, I crossed the Nullarbor in a day and a night. Finally, I made it to Adelaide, where I was dropped in an industrial suburb at 3 am, with nowhere to stay. I found a railway line and walked along it for a bit. There was nothing else to do. In one direction I could see the faint light of a railway station, the other just a continuation of fuck-all and a bend. I walked along the line towards the station, trying to step from sleeper to sleeper. The station was dead.

What next? I pondered, mooching back down the way I'd come. I scouted around for a spot to sleep. This was as close as I'd come to being a bum. I felt as if I belonged in Steinbeck's *The Grapes of Wrath*. Not much money and sleeping rough, but I liked the feeling. I found a suitable flat spot to lay out my mat and I took it. I flattened the grass down around me, and used the torch to look for ants or other creepy crawlies. I prayed for no spiders. Satisfied, I slept, the sort of sleep where I continually awoke, expecting the foot of a pissed eighteen-year-old to come crashing into my face.

I opened my eyes in the morning to the sound of a train rattling past on its way to the city centre. A lone passenger sat staring out the window at what he must have thought was a homeless bum. I gave him a little homeless wave from my sleeping bag and he smiled.

The sun was well on its way and the freshness of the morning light had faded. I packed up my stuff, headed off to the station and caught a suburban train into Adelaide.

I next caught a bus out to the edge of the highway that led to Victoria. Needing a quick poo, I walked into a nearby Bunnings hardware store. Early morning shoppers were picking out the best outdoor settings, perusing drill bits, testing grinding wheels and drinking Bunnings coffee, and they all paused to stare at the incongruity of a tall man with a backpack strolling through their suburban dreams. I felt far away from their lives and miles away from my own. I felt like the outsider I'd chosen to become, the pointless meanderer, the traveller, and it all felt good. It gave an arrogance to my strut and a haughtiness to my grin.

In the toilets, I stripped down to my underpants and gave myself a bit of a wash in the hand basin. When I walked back out on the road I felt more at home, like the roadside was my companion. I smelt good, too.

Once on the highway I knew I could be home by the end of the day if things went well. To me that meant home-cooked meals, showers, jokes with family, warm beds and Mum's Milo. I stared down the hill at the oncoming traffic, which was steady for a Sunday, so I popped my thumb out with reasonable optimism. After twenty minutes or so, I noticed a car was travelling towards me with an occupant rapidly winding down their window. I was in for a verbal volley. A woman of about twenty-five leaned out the window, her scraggly blonde locks roaring around her head like she was Medusa.

'Get a job, you fucking, dole-bludging cunt,' she screamed.

I didn't make eye contact with her at all. I was already looking at the car behind, eyeballing them for a lift. No point paying attention to somebody who wasn't going to take me anywhere. It meant a little more than that, though. I still wanted to get home.

25
Armor Alled

Two friendly heads beamed at me. Once their car pulled over, a 50-year-old man jumped out.

'We'll chuck that in the boot, mate,' he said to me, referring to my gear. 'Where are you off to?'

'Ballarat. Thanks a lot for stopping.'

'No worries at all. Jump in. I'm Darrell.'

I jumped into the back of the Holden, which by the look of the interior was a Statesman. The super-plush seats appeared well cared for. Everything was shiny. It even smelt shiny. I'd been travelling with little sleep for a long time and it occurred to me that the seats were so lovely I wanted to lick them.

'This is Lorraine, John. She's my beautiful wife.'

'G'day, Lorraine. How you going?'

'I'm going well,' said Lorraine.

In my head I was still contemplating licking the seat. I wondered if Lorraine would have still been 'going well' if I'd begun lapping at her head-rest like a dehydrated cat.

Lorraine and Darrell had come from a wedding where the bridal party were transported around in trucks. I'd never heard of that happening before. I liked the idea. It reminded me of Joe saying, 'That's a fucking stupid idea', when I told him of my dream to have a truck as a runabout. But I thought Darrell and Lorraine would support such a concept. 'So where have you come from, John?' asked Lorraine.

'I've just hitchhiked a lap of Australia and this is my last leg.'

'A full lap of Australia?'

Most people responded incredulously to my feat, which was pleasing, but I knew I'd achieved nothing. I was an anachronism, like a guy in a bar with an Elvis haircut. I'd done something five thousand people probably did in the seventies. Not amazing at all.

'Well done, John. Did you have a lot of fun?' asked Lorraine.

'I saw a heap of road signs and truckers' bum cracks,' I replied.

Both Darrell and Lorraine let out a laugh as if I were a naughty nephew of the sort who becomes a favoured nut because he does 'weird things' like eating sausages with mustard instead of tomato sauce. I imagined them whispering to one another in such a situation: 'Yeah, I think it was mustard …'

'Mustard … oh God. You just can't explain some people.'

I figured they had behavioural boundaries typical of white Australian suburbia. There was a small amount of *Kath and Kim* going on. I loved it.

Lorraine and Darrell told me they lived in 'the Marsh' – Bacchus Marsh – which excited me because I grew up in nearby Greendale.

'The Marsh!' I exclaimed. 'Awesome. Mum used to buy our shoes there. I mean my brothers' and sisters' and my shoes there. At Nigel's. You know him?'

'Yes, we know him,' said Lorraine. We bought school shoes for our boys there, didn't we, Darrell?'

It appeared 'the Marsh' was the world capital for school shoes.

'What about Russell's? Did you shop there?' I asked them.

'Yes we did,' replied. Good shop that, Russell's. Plenty of variety.'

I was definitely overtired. At this rate the next question I'd ask was likely to be, 'Which public toilets were your favourite? The ones near Toy Kingdom or the ones near the hospital?'

Lorraine and Darrell had four boys. They were all successful in their eyes, but they described one of them as being a bit different. I pondered the possibilities: gay hairdresser, contemporary dancer, Jesus freak or a combination of all of them. It turned out he worked in a skateboard shop. Not that different. I wondered how they would describe him if he worked at Bras n' Things. I quickly forgot what the others did but there were wives, cars, boats, campers and all that Aussie stuff.

Darrell's phone rang to snap me out of my mind-mush.

'Yerp. Hello. Bob, how you going?' He paused then answered, 'Good mate. No worries here.'

Darrell's tone indicated that he might have to work.

I was right. Bob was his boss and Darrell was being asked to drive a truck later that day. Bob was trying to find out when Darrell would be back.

'I don't know if I can get there by five, mate,' Darrell said.

'Why not?' I overheard Bob say.

'I gotta pull over and give Lorraine a quickie.'

Lorraine screwed up her face and punched Darrell on the arm. Darrell was laughing his head off, as was I. Lorraine even arced up laughing.

Bob got to the point. 'So will you be here by five, Darrell?'

'Oh, I don't know mate ... might just have to give her a quickie.'

And the laughter started again. Apparently saying 'give her a quickie' was the funniest line available to humanity. To be fair, I laughed the hardest, but I'd had only about four hours sleep in the last two days. I was a little delirious.

As the morning passed we neared the South Australia–
Victoria border. When it was time for lunch, Lorraine and
Darrell talked of all the different possibilities.

'What about Kaniva, Darrell, what's the food like there?'
asked Lorraine.

'It's not bad, Lorraine. Good chips,' replied Darrell.

'What do you reckon then?' she said.

'Or … I don't know.'

'What about Nhill, is that any good?' continued Lorraine.

'Yeah it's nice. Most of the food along here is good
enough.'

I began to see the subtext. Lorraine was saying, 'I'm proud of
you for knowing the best truck stops on the Western Highway.
I'm proud that you've toiled up and down to make a living for
our family.' It was cute.

'Dimboola's the go, sweetie,' Darrell finally decided. 'Good
burgers in the truck stop in Dimboola.'

'That sounds like the go then, Darrell. What do you reckon,
John, Dimboola?'

'Sounds great.'

'Darrell, you know all the good spots, don't you, love?'
Lorraine said.

'Aw, I don't know about that. I don't know about that.'

'You do.'

'Dunno 'bout that.'

Lunch in Dimboola was pretty tasty, but the chips Darrell had ordered did not arrive.

'I think they've forgotten your chips, Darrell,' said Lorraine.

'Yeah, I think they have,' said Darrell.

'I'll ask,' offered Lorraine.

'Stay there. I'll do it, love.'

It turned out they'd forgotten the chips. However, Darrell and Lorraine didn't complain. They got their money back for the chips and left. No fuss. It's funny and perhaps generational, but complaining now seems to be a national pastime. I love it when people just get on with it. They see past errors and focus on the good things that surround them.

All along the highway, Darrell and Lorraine were positive, pointing out cool things. They even stopped to take a photo of a fake Santa stuck in a tinsel-covered ute. They loved it.

'Sarah's gonna love this,' Lorraine stated.

'Yeah, she'll think it's superfluous,' Darrell retorted.

'Oh yes,' said Lorraine.

I think Darrell meant superlative, but superfluous bizarrely fitted. I think tinsel-covered utes with Santas in them are superfluous. Verbal fuck-ups like that had happened a few times on my journey around our great nation. I got the feeling that people thought they needed to use big words because I was a teacher. Every so often lift-givers would push the limits of their vocabulary, as if to say, 'Don't worry

about me, mate. I know what's going on.' Well, it was
superfluous.

Every now and again you come across people like Lorraine
and Darrell. Whoever raised them did a wonderful job. Their
manners, attitude and dashboard were all in immaculate
condition. It was as if they had Armor Alled their car and all
facets of their spirits and personalities.

26
Dad

Lorraine and Darrel dropped me at the off-ramp into Ballarat. I was dizzily tired and forgot their names for the last hour and a half of my journey. About a minute before I left the car, I remembered.

'See ya, Lorraine. See ya, Darrell. Thanks again.'

'See ya, John. All the best,' they said in unison.

I walked to a spot that had been predetermined by a series of texts to my sister. I was almost at the end of my journey, and I'd arranged for my family to meet me at Ballarat, not far from our family home in the countryside. The family weren't there waiting. My heart sank a little. It was like completing the Sydney to Hobart yacht race and arriving at an empty finish line.

After some brief phone calls they arrived. I'd been waiting in the wrong spot. That was the problem.

Ruth, Mary and Dad were all in the car: two sisters and a father. Whatever was being said, the atmosphere was just family. I presumed they'd been arguing about my location because I'd said things on the phone like, 'I'm near some pine trees.' Not exact advice.

Hanging out with family is amazing because whatever the mood is, you slide in as if you're still in the prime of your adolescence. It was awesome to see them. They carted me home via the bottle shop where I bought a few triumphant beers. It was good to talk to people who I didn't have to be extra nice to. To prove the point, I farted loudly in the car.

'Johnny! Jeeesuss!'

'Just Jesus will be fine,' I said.

Mum cooked steak that night and I loved it. But what I really loved was being able to open the pantry cupboard and raid it.

I told my old man that I hadn't finished my lap of the country yet.

'But you're back,' he said.

'No, I've got to get to Melbourne to finish,' I told him.

'No, you don't. Don't be ridiculous.'

'I'll hitchhike tomorrow out the front there. You'll pick me up, yeah?'

'No way. Catch a train,' he said.

'Come on, Dad,' I pleaded.

'It's ridiculous.'

'Just to Melbourne. It ain't far.'

'Alright, Jesus. We'll leave early.'

'Terrific.'

It seemed to make sense. The whole hitchhiking adventure was partially inspired by my Dad's adventurous spirit, so the fucker should've at least given me a lift, I reckoned.

The next morning I walked to the end of the driveway and stood on the road with my thumb out, much like Dad had done when he was a young man. He drove out the gate and pulled over next to me. Earlier that morning I'd told him that he'd be driving me all the way to Melbourne – a journey of about an hour – while pretending he didn't know me. I'd also pretend not to know him.

He picked me up and I greeted my father. 'How you going there, mate?' I asked as I hopped in the car, half giggling.

'Fighting fit! You?'

'Good, mate. John's my name.'

'I'm Allan.'

I thought this was all pretty funny. My dad was a smashing actor, a side of him I'd hardly ever seen.

'Where are you going, Allan? I'm sorry, was it Allan?'

'Yes. Allan. I'm going to Melbourne.'

'Oh fantastic, that's where I'm going, Allan. Was that it, Allan? Allan.'

He was staying right in character despite my idiocy.

'Have you done much hitching yourself, mate?' I asked. I already knew the stories he'd tell me, but it didn't matter.

'Yes, John. I've done quite a bit.'

'Whereabouts?'

'Iran, Turkey, Israel, Germany, all over Europe. South Africa, Canada.'

'Wow. What was it like hitching in Turkey and Israel?'

'I started in Turkey after hitching in Europe with a friend of mine called Chris Willy.'

'You're not making names up, are you, Allan?' He ignored my joke and ploughed on.

'Chris Willy and I were camping on a beach in Turkey and a Turkish fellow told us of another couple of Englishmen in Mersin, not too far away,' Dad explained. 'It would seem strange nowadays to be told this, but not many people visited Turkey in those days so it was expected that we should meet them. So we went to Mersin. Their names were John Kane and Roy Warne. They were nice chaps and talked of going to Haifa in Israel. Both Chris and I thought it a good idea, so together we decided that we'd try hitching a ride on a ship. The next day we took off down to the port and organised with a shipping agent to catch a sugar ship called the *Pal Yam* across to Israel. The shipping agent told

us that there would be two Swiss girls on the boat with us as
well.'

'Did you root them, Allan?'

'Ah, ha ha ha. They were nice girls.'

'Does that mean you rooted them, everyone rooted them or
none of you rooted them?'

'We got to Israel within a day or two.' I'd been ignored. 'John
Kane was a religious zealot and we were in Israel, so of course he
told us he knew somebody we could stay with,' Dad continued.
'That took a couple of days to arrange, so in the meantime we
stayed on the *Pal Yam*. John ended up staying in the house for
six weeks, but Chris and I decided to hitch down to the Red Sea
coast to a place called Eilat. We decided that it should be a
hitchhiking race.'

'A race? Grouse.'

'We looked for a lift at the port and boarded a couple of
ships to ask the captains for passage. We were both escorted from
the port by the Israeli Army.'

'*Jesus!*' I replied. 'They could've thought you were Hamas
spies. You look pretty hairy, Allan.' Ignored again.

'In the end we both managed to get to Eilat and back without
too many concerns.'

'Who won, you or Chris Willy?'

'I can't remember, actually.'

'Come on, you're just being modest, Allan. You won.'

'I really don't know.'

I hoped Dad won. I didn't want some guy with the same name as a cock beating him. 'You won,' I repeated, slipping slightly out of character.

'After that, I picked up work for three weeks as a film extra. I was in a film called *Judith*, starring Peter Finch and Sophia Loren.'

'Did you root Sophia Loren?' I'd asked Dad this question nearly every Christmas for twenty years. He'd never said no, but he'd never said yes. In fact he never said anything. I hope he knobbed her.

'The film was a flop, apparently.'

'Where'd you go next?'

'Chris and Roy went their separate ways so John and I decided to go back to Istanbul.'

'You and the religious nut?'

'Yes. Well, no. John Kane, who is religious, and I.'

'Do you love Jesus too, Allan?'

'We jumped on a Turkish ship.' Ignored yet again. 'But before we got on, one of the sailors asked if we could carry a suitcase to an address in Istanbul in exchange for accommodation.'

'Fair dinkum?' I didn't remember this part of the story from when he'd told me previously.

'We took it.'

'You're fucking joking me, Allan. You're a bloody drug runner.'

'We never looked in it, so I'll never know. But we stayed in the accommodation at Istanbul for a couple of days.'

'A drug dealer's house! You're like Pablo Escabar.' I couldn't believe how dumb my dad had been. But on second thoughts I figured that, in those days, they didn't have shows like *Customs* or *Border Protection* to wise them up. At that time the Bali Nine weren't even in a ball sack yet.

'From Turkey,' Dad went on, 'John and I decided to hitchhike to Tehran in Iran.'

'Iran? Well, that is ridiculous.'

I was trying to stay in character, assuming people would think hitchhiking in Iran was ridiculous. Dad was going well holding character as we went past 'the Marsh' on our way to Melbourne.

'It was a ten-day hitchhike, most of which was spent in snow. For three weeks, John and I had numb feet.'

'Holy fuck. Frostbite?'

'No, luckily for us.'

'What was it like out there?'

'Pretty rural. At one point we were told to come inside a small hut. Through sign language we were asked why we were not carrying a gun.'

'What?'

'They were telling us there were wolves around and it wasn't safe without a gun. Anyway, we got to Iran and visited my brother's friend, Geoff Smythe. I ended up staying for six months, teaching English to the super-rich. John got meningitis and had to return home.'

'Didn't you get sick too?' Whoops, I dropped character. 'Umm ... did you get sick, Allan?'

'Yes, John, I did. Just before I was due to go back to Istanbul and then to Munich. I travelled for five days on buses and trains with fully blown hepatitis.'

'Well done, Allan. Did you root anyone on the train? A German? The train conductor? Anyone? Your stories have no sex, Allan.'

'I am not a pervert, John.'

'Are you saying I am?'

'Jump to your own conclusions.'

'I am, you're right. But I am your son.'

'You're a hitchhiker. You're nobody's son.'

With that, we laughed and dropped character. We talked about Hawthorn's prospects for the season ahead. That was the sort of talk I'd missed the most. Regular stuff.

27
Final

I used to think that Australians were ungenerous and quick to whinge. I was wrong. Aussies will bend over backwards for somebody in need.

In Victoria, after the 2009 bushfires, people built better homes than the ones that had been burnt down. Australians chipped in over $115 million. Such a sentiment of generosity was something I was privileged enough to feel when hitchhiking. The number of times people offered to buy me lunch, put me up, run me miles out of their way, or drive different routes to check out local attractions and give me a discount was ridiculous. There were also people who bought me beer, talked freely about personal things, gave me tips about where to stay, arranged my next lift or tried to give me something they owned. Reminiscing about that fills my heart with joy. I've been to a few other countries in the world and I've found that, in comparison to the rest of my experiences, Australians are very generous to each other.

Take Joe, for example. Joe picked me up off the road and drove me 2000 kilometres through the desert. He offered to put me up in his home for a 'few days'. He told me to ride his motorbike down to the south coast of Western Australia. I didn't really know this man.

Between 2002 and 2004 I lived in England. I got to know some people really well, people I came to love to death. Not one of them ever offered me the use of their vehicle, even for a day. There is a real come-and-share philosophy in Australia. I felt it, I know it and I loved it.

If you suspect that you are in this book, you may be right, but I have changed your name. Using real names would possibly have caused my assets to be seized in a law dispute by some jaded truck driver. (All they'd have gained, though, would be 23 CDs and a small bag of Lego.) I changed names because people told me about their lives in confidence and I didn't tell them I was going to write it all down. People told me things that they'd hate their wife, parents, brothers, sisters, kids, cousins, congregation, associates, neighbours, dog, cat, chickens and grandparents to know. Many of those same people also told me things their relatives, friends, family, bosses, dogs, etc, would've loved to know. One can't come without the other.

And what of me? Despite the disappointment of WAAPA, I was still keen on a career in radio, with the course at Swinburne still a possibility. I also wanted to pursue writing and, hopefully, get my work published. I'd taken six months out of my life to try to achieve these two goals.

After returning home from hitchhiking, I spent the early part of the summer in a drunken lament, wondering if things would ever swing my way.

Then my life changed.

I was standing in the kitchen with Laura one day when the phone rang. It was a number I didn't recognise.

'Hello, John Card speaking.'

'Hello, John. It's James from Swinburne University.'

'Oh, how you going, James?' My mind fired in a million directions. Was it possible?

'Fine. I'm just letting you know that you got into the Radio Broadcasting course.'

You faarkin' beauty! Yes, yes, yesss. That's great news, James. Thanks for letting me know.'

'I'm glad you're pleased, John.'

'Pleased? I'm fucking rapt!'

My summer lament washed away. I'd achieved something. Skipping out on teaching to kick at least one goal out of two had been achieved. Laura and I power-hugged in celebration, then I let go and bounced around the kitchen, hooting.

During the year that it took to complete my radio course, I lived with a mate called Patto in Melbourne and taught in high schools to pay the bills. Teaching was a vacuum that continually drew me in. I also kept chipping away at my writing, attempting to make the material presentable to a publisher. Writing was the most unrealistic dream I've ever conjured, but it was far too much fun to ignore. I'd be working at private schools with classes full of boys in front of me, typing my manuscript and reliving the experiences in my head. I'd travelled around what my mother liked to call the 'real Australia', and it's not anything like the Australia such privileged children had been born into. So I'd say, 'Pens down, look at me, yes, you there with the red hair, look up, that's it … I've got a story to tell you guys.'

Joe was often my first port of call, because I was keen to let them know that people who look crazy aren't always so. Sometimes I'd read them a bullying story. For these kids, there was incongruity in hearing about me getting bullied, as I'm now quite a tall man and weigh 90 kilograms. But I liked to make the point that it can happen to anyone and that you can get past it. When I told classes about my teenage run-ins with Tank, my guts would twist into a knot, my voice would quaver and the dam wall just behind my eyes would begin to tremble at the pressure. There was something about telling kids bullying stories that I really enjoyed. The impact it had on them was obvious.

I spent 2011 working for a radio station in central NSW, talking shit to Aussies for a living. My start in radio didn't turn out the way I'd envisaged, but those stories are for later. At that time, I couldn't believe what I had achieved. My life up to the point where I took off around Australia had felt directionless, pointless and meandering. The long waits on the road had shown me that, with patience and persistence, the destination will come. In Victoria River, when I was roasting in the shade of a tree, feeling lonely and staring at the empty tarmac, I remembered saying to myself, *It will come John, just keep smiling up the road.* The next lift took me 1000 kilometres to Broome.

Sometimes the light that you throw out into the world will come flying back at you and sometimes it dissipates in a puddle of hate. I learned to try and hang onto those periods of light. Draw them out, make them longer, even when the multitudes of negativity come to rip it apart. 'Doing whatever' is not a solution.

My hitchhike had fired me up, given me optimism, motivation and a love for humanity. It demanded that I stand tall when the shit hit the fan, something I'd missed throughout my twenties. I worry for young people making the same mistakes I did: wasting time, plodding. Waiting this long to live a life I should've been living when I was 23 was a mistake. And now, you're reading my story, that manuscript I worked away at while teaching. I now understand what it's like to pursue and achieve a dream. It feels fucking ace.

I encourage others to live their dreams at every opportunity. Before this adventure I thought my own dreams were all unachievable yet I motored on anyway, trying to make them a reality. It's this persistence that led to change. Ignoring doomsayers and negative nancies is the hardest part in working towards your goals. You must believe in your own dream, nothing else. Nobody has anything to gain from sitting on their hopes.

Other great memoirs by Finch

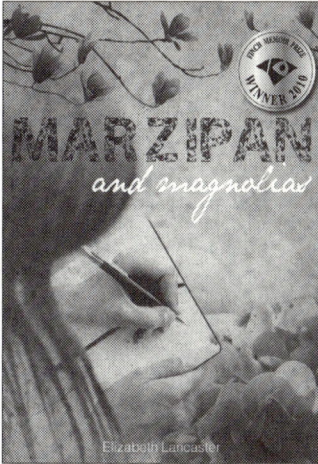

Marzipan & Magnolias
Elizabeth Lancaster
ISBN: 9781921462207

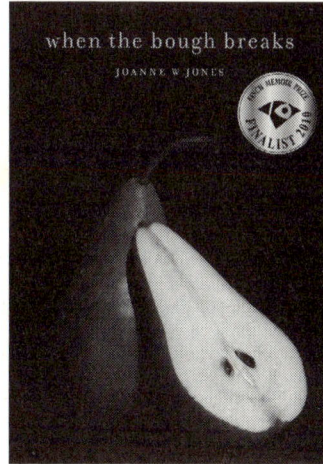

When the Bough Breaks
Joanne W Jones
ISBN: 9781921462221

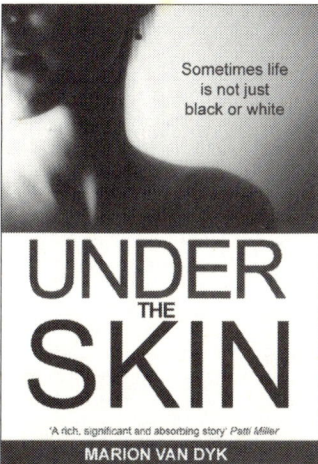

Under the Skin
Marion van Dyk
ISBN:9781921462801

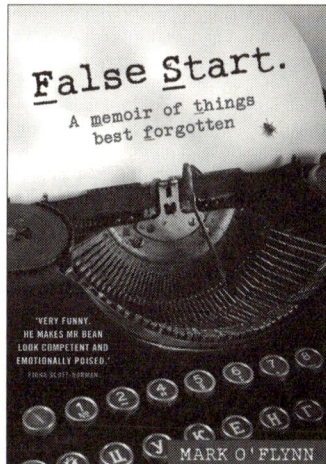

False Start
Mark O'Flynn
ISBN:9781921462894

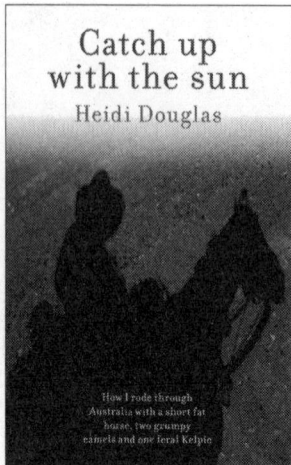

Catch Up With the Sun
Heidi Douglas
ISBN:9781921462368

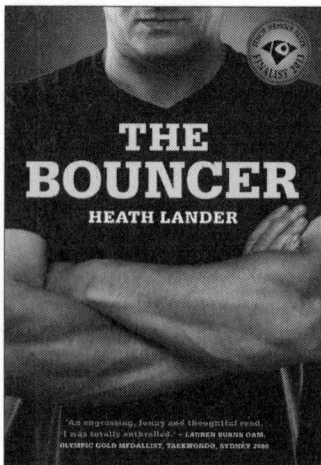

The Bouncer
Heath Lander
ISBN:9780987419651

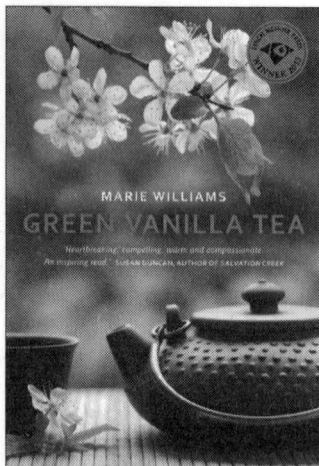

Green Vanilla Tea
Marie Williams
ISBN: 9781921462993

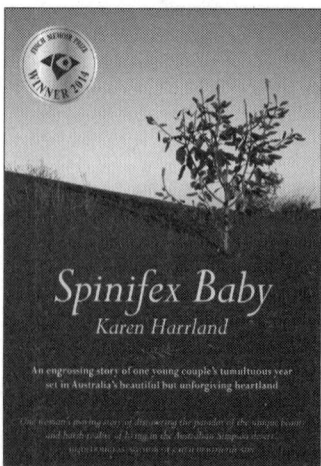

Spinifex Baby
Karen Harrland
ISBN: 9781925048155